Introduction

This short course is meant to provide an Introduction to the Capitular Degrees for those who have decided to take the next step on Freemasonry, following the Three Blue Lodge Degrees.

There are many excellent books about the symbolism of the Chapter, but many of them are about the English (or so-called 'Domatic') system, and don't make easy reading for an American reader. There are also number of impressive Monitors, written by great men and Masons. Thomas Smith Webb and Albert Gallatin Mackey are but two of these luminaries. However, again these serve more as reference books to those who are already familiar with the Rituals and their meaning.

It is hoped that this book fills the gap for the modern Companion who needs a little help to understand the Capitular environment. For this reason this course, in addition to giving an overview of the Degrees, also looks at practical topics, such as the organization of a Chapter, Grand Chapter, the Constitutions, the Charities, and General Grand Chapter.

I would like to thank the Educational Committee for their support, and in particular Griffith Jones III for pointing me towards working on Capitular education in the first place; Edmund D. Harrison, Jeffrey M. Williamson and 'R.J.' Kessler for their advice and encouragement; John D. Samuel for his tireless proofreading and suggestions; and especially Jason P. Sheridan for his seemingly endless support of all my hair-brained schemes!

Notwithstanding, all errors in fact or spelling are mine alone.

Piers A. Vaughan
February 2014

Introduction to Capitular Masonry
Piers A. Vaughan
© Rose Circle Publications
Pub. Feb. 2014
ISBN 978-0-9815421-0-2

Grand Chapter State of New York, Royal Arch Masons

This Course has been approved by the Grand High Priest

M∴E∴ Richard J. Kessler

by the Grand Lecturer

R∴E∴ Peter Pizzorno

and by the

2013 Royal Arch Masonic Education Committee

R∴E∴ Piers A. Vaughan
R∴E∴ Alan M. Bryant
R∴E∴ John Lenza
M∴E∴ Jeffrey M. Williamson

This Course was prepared by:

R∴E∴ Piers A. Vaughan
Grand King
Grand Chapter State of New York, Royal Arch Masons
January 2014

Table of Contents

The Purpose of *Introduction to Capitular Masonry*

This course is intended to give those who have been elected to membership in a Chapter a basic understanding of the organization they have joined. This includes a brief review of the history of Capitular Masonry, and a high level review of some of the key points in each of the four Degrees. By the end of the Course the participants should have a broad understanding of the Chapter Degrees, and feel comfortable with the activities in the Chapter Room. We hope this knowledge will both encourage them to attend their Chapter regularly, and in time take an Office in Chapter.

The course also looks at some of the other aspects of Capitular Masonry, including the structure and organization of Chapters and Grand Chapter; and a brief review of the Charities associated with the Grand Chapter of the State of New York, Royal Arch Masons.

Following the completion of the Degrees, the first meeting the newly-made Companion attends should be the Chapter Walkabout Ceremony, included in this Course, and also listed separately on the website (ny-royal-arch.org).

It draws its inspiration from the excellent LSOME course developed by the Grand Lodge of Free & Accepted Masons of the State of New York.

The course is to be run within each Chapter by a competent Facilitator. At least two or three other Companions should attend to give a broader spectrum of ideas and opinions during the discussions with the new members. There should be three to four Sessions; one following each Degree (although Session 2 and 3 can be run together following the Virtual Past Master and Most Excellent Master Degrees), as soon as possible after each Degree. Following the last session the next Chapter meeting should be the Chapter Walkabout Ceremony.

Copies of this course are available in paperback format for a fee, or for no charge in PDF format on applying to the Grand Chapter offices at grandram@aol.com or by going to the Educational section at ny-royal-arch.org.

Session 1
(Following the Mark Master Degree)

INTRODUCTION

The first meeting introduces the Candidate to the first step beyond the first three Degrees, and explains the two main branches of Freemasonry, the York and the Scottish Rites. Focusing on the York Rite, following a brief history the session examines how two old Degrees were fused together to form this honorary Degree. The sessions concludes by emphasizing some of the key symbols used, and links them back to the Blue Lodge Degrees.

FIRST SESSION SUBJECTS

1. The York Rite and the Scottish Rite
2. A Little History
3. The Mark Man and Mark Master Degree
4. Key Symbols in the Mark Master Degree

THE YORK RITE AND THE SCOTTISH RITE

Welcome to the Introduction to Capitular Masonry! We are delighted that you have decided to continue your Masonic journey with us. Many people become Freemasons and yet never continue their experience or education beyond the first three Degrees of Blue Lodge. This is a pity, because there is so much more to learn and enjoy in what are sometimes referred to as at 'Higher Degrees.' however, do not be fooled: these Degrees are only 'higher' in terms of their number. There is nothing in Masonry higher than the Master Mason Degree. So while the Royal Arch Degrees are numbered 4 through 7, they are simply a continuation of the education you first received in the Blue Lodge.

There are two main branches of Freemasonry beyond the Blue Lodge: the Scottish Rite and the York Rite.

The York Rite consists of four parts: the Lodge, the Chapter, the Council and the Commandery.

The Lodge (or Blue Lodge) meets under the authority of the Grand Master of the State, and is authorized to confer the Entered Apprentice, Fellowcraft and Master Masons Degrees.

The Chapter meetings under the authority of the Grand Chapter of the State, and confers the Mark Master, Virtual Past Master, Most Excellent Master and Holy Royal Arch Degrees.

The Council meets under the authority of the Grand Cryptic Council of the State, and confers the Royal Master, Select Master and Superexcellent Master Degrees.

The Commandery confers the Chivalric Orders, being the Order of the Red Cross, the Order of Malta and the Order of the Temple (also known as the Masonic Knights Templar).

The four Degrees of the Royal Arch system will expand your understanding of the Blue Lodge Degrees. Here you will learn how to receive your wages, referred to in the Senior Warden's words at the Opening; why King Solomon and King Hiram could not give the True Word of Master Mason; the identifying characteristics of a Worshipful Master; and finally the True Word of Master Mason!

And so, congratulations on joining those who continue to seek more Light in Masonry; who strive to make that 'daily advancement in Masonic knowledge'; and who have taken that further step to become one of those fortunate Masons who have embarked on what is a lifetime study of human philosophy and ancient esoteric wisdom.

I has been said that we are bound to our Brothers through our Lodge; but we choose our Companions. Thank you for choosing us as your Companions through life!

The Scottish Rite takes its origins from mainland Europe - particularly France. It is called Scottish (or in French *écossaise*) because it is associated with the exiled court of King James II of Scotland and England, who was expelled from England in 1688, mainly because he attempted to reestablish Roman Catholicism as the official religion there. He and his descendants, including Bonnie Prince Charlie, signed Masonic Charters while in exile in France. Partly out of loyalty to this exiled Royal family, the series of Degrees developed outside of mainstream English Masonry became known as the Scottish Degrees. Although there were many different systems, they eventually coalesced around Bordeaux into what would be called the Scottish Rite, from where they traveled West, firstly to the Caribbean, and eventually to the United States via Charleston, NC.

The York Rite is also known as the American Rite. Although it romantically links its Degrees to the legends of an early Lodge in York, England, in fact most of the Degrees beyond the Blue Lodge Degrees were never administered by a single Grand Body in England, and even now the United Grand Lodge of England only lays claim to the first three Degrees (including the Royal Arch Degree). All the others found in the American Rite are administered through several independent sovereign bodies. Here in the United States, the York Rite actually commences with the Blue Lodge Degrees, continues through the four Royal Arch Degrees and the three Cryptic Degrees, and ends with the Chivalric Orders of the Red Cross, Malta and the Order of the Temple.

Note that the Scottish Rite is a system of 33 Degrees, including the first three Degrees. However, by common agreement, since the Blue Lodge Degrees are under the control of the Grand Lodges of each State, and the Grand Master has control of all Orders in his State in most jurisdictions, the first three Degrees of the Scottish Rite are never performed in the vast majority of jurisdictions. Therefore the Blue Lodge Degrees are claimed by the York Rite, which is why the Mark Master Degree is seen as the fourth Degree in the system, and so on.

The Royal Arch Degrees are also called the Capitular Degrees. This is because the Royal Arch is conferred in a Chapter. The word comes from the Latin *capitulum*, meaning chapter, which was mainly used to refer to an assembly of Roman Catholic, and Protestant canons, or any high ranking clergy. In the past few hundred years the word has gained popularity as an assembly of like-minded people united in a common cause, and it was perhaps inevitable, given the tradition of identifying the origin of Freemasonry with the Masonic bands who built the cathedrals and chapels, that the word 'Chapter' would come to be used to designate a group of Masons. Indeed, in the broad family of Masonic Orders we can find mention of Lodges, Chapters, Colleges, Preceptories, Commanderies, Consistories, Chapels, Assemblages, Temples, Councils and Conclaves, to name just a few.

A LITTLE HISTORY

In 2013 the Supreme Grand Chapter of England celebrated its 200th Anniversary. However, this does not reflect the true age of the Holy Royal Arch. This event celebrated the Act of Union, when the Antients and Moderns joined together to form a United Grand Lodge. The history of the Royal Arch Degree - and the Mark Degree for that matter - goes back at least as far as the Entered Apprentice and Fellowcraft Degrees.

The high esteem in which the Holy Royal Arch was held can be seen in the famous statement of Laurence Dermott, who was Grand Secretary of the Antients' Grand Lodge, that the Degree was the "root, heart and marrow of Freemasonry."

The story of the Holy Royal Arch and the Second Temple is so popular it is found in many different Masonic Degree systems, originating in England, Scotland, Ireland and even in France. It is also a pre-requisite for membership in a large number of Masonic Orders. This is not merely an arbitrary requirement: the Degree is considered to be the completion of the Sublime Degree of Master Mason Degree, which could be considered to have an inconclusive ending. The Royal Arch is therefore seen to complete a cycle, and the so-called 'Higher Degrees' begin a new one, whether by telling a new story, like the Cryptic Degrees, or covering a later historical period, such as the Order of the Temple.

When the Premier Grand Lodge was founded in 1717, the main focus of those four Lodges was to restore the tradition of holding Quarterly Communications, and honoring the Saints John Days with banquets. However, this presupposes that Lodges were already in existence, and if there was any intent of standardizing the Rituals being practiced by creating a central governing body, this was certainly not one of its original stated purposes. Indeed, to begin with the Grand Lodge only held sway over four Lodges, and had no interest in regulating those Lodges which met outside the bounds of the capital city. Unfortunately, records from that time are scarce, and even Grand Lodge records are missing for the first six years, until the first Grand Secretary was appointed in 1723.

There is a continuing debate over whether the Royal Arch ever formed part of the Third Degree. One side says it did, but was removed from the ritual since Masonry was seen as a supporter of the House of Stuart, which had been expelled from England and replaced by the House of Hanover, best known for the succession of Kings George I through IV. The theory says that, in order to survive, Freemasonry had to reinvent itself. This it did by creating a Grand Lodge, completely rewriting the Third Degree (traditional history tells us that the Master Mason Degree did not appear until the 1720s or 1730s), and scheming to attract a Patron from the Hanoverian Royal family. The other side says there was never any connection between the Master Mason Degree and the Holy Royal Arch, and that the latter was simply one of many independent Degrees which were circulating around the unregulated country prior to the establishment of the Premier Grand Lodge. Such Degrees also included the Mark Degree.

Masonry probably came to the American colonies at a very early time. Just because the Premier Grand Lodge starting to charter Lodges in England, and later in France, Germany and then the colonies, does not mean that many early Lodges weren't self-chartering or that they didn't practice a variety of rituals. Indeed, it was quite common for Masons to be given authority or claim authority to confer Degrees - sometimes for a fee - and to establish Lodges. Some Lodges such as St. John's Lodge No. 1 were formally chartered by the Premier Grand Lodge. But it is highly likely that Masons from other unregulated parts of England brought with them their own local Rituals and claimed authority. People were also emigrating from Scotland, Ireland and mainland Europe, so the range of Rituals grew over time.

A second complication arose from the establishment of the Grand Lodge of the Antients in 1751, which lost no time in chartering both fixed Lodges in England and traveling Lodges in the military services, who brought these Lodges to the colonies, setting up local Lodges under their authority. Independent Royal Arch No. 2, is believed to have been originally so chartered. Being so far from the battles between the Antients and the Moderns in England, these several types of Lodge interacted amicably enough: after all, there were more important matters to be concerned about!

As an aside it is interesting to note that the first record of the Royal Arch Degree being worked in the American colonies is at Fredericksburg Lodge, Virginia: the very Lodge in which George Washington was Initiated, Passed and Raised. Was George Washington a Royal Arch Mason? No definitive documentary evidence has been found. However, some scholars point out that some near contemporary engravings of George Washington as a Mason contain symbols unique to the Royal Arch. Whether this is artistic license, or an indication that he was indeed a Companion, is a matter of intense debate.

During the Revolutionary War activity among Lodges in general subsided. However, at the conclusion of the war in 1783, Masonic activity resumed with a vengeance, and even Washington's Inauguration and first President was planned and executed by a number of prominent Masons, including Chancellor Livingston, who was also Grand Master of New York, and General Jacob Morton, Master of St. John's Lodge No.1. Even Samuel Fraunces, proprietor of Faunces' Tavern and Washington's Steward for his first year living in New York, was initiated into Holland Lodge No. 8 mere weeks before the Inauguration.

During the 1780s a number of Chapters came into existence, some styling themselves Grand Chapters. In New York the Grand Chapter of the State of New York, Royal Arch Masons was chartered by the General Grand Chapter - whose ink was still wet on its own self-Charter - on March 14, 1798. The only older Grand Chapters are Rhode Island and Massachusetts, which beat

New York by one and two days respectively; and the Grand Chapter of Pennsylvania, which was previously chartered by its Grand Lodge twenty-eight months earlier, on November 30, 1795.

One of American Masonry's current concerns is the issue of One Day Classes; whether they help to grow the Craft and whether the retention rate among one-day Masons is high enough to justify the practice. Another question is the issue of seeing young Masons accelerate through the Offices of their Blue Lodge, and indeed joining the Concordant Bodies as soon as they receive their Master Mason Degree. It is interesting to note that both practices have existed since the earliest days of Freemasonry. For example, St. John's Lodge No. 1 has copious minutes documenting the conferring of all three Degree upon men in one or two days, prior to their setting sail from New York harbor; and one of the greatest luminaries in the popularity of Royal Arch Masonry, Thomas Smith Webb, was initiated into Freemasonry on December 17, 1790, when he was barely 20 years old. And he was instrumental in establishing the General Grand Chapter, the body which was set up to oversee the Grand Chapters of the various States in 1789 at the tender age of 29 - indeed the same age as DeWitt Clinton when he became Grand High Priest of the State of New York, prior to becoming the General Grand High Priest of General Grand Chapter! We will learn more about these Grand bodies later on.

At this point it is sufficient to recognize that Thomas Smith Webb worked tirelessly to standardize the work. The Rituals he edited and embellished are essentially those we use today.

New York Companions can be justly proud that they are members of not only one of the oldest Grand Chapters in the world; but which also produced the most influential characters in Royal Arch Masonry in America!

THE MARK MAN AND MARK MASTER DEGREE

The origin of the Mark Degree, like that of the regular Blue Degrees, is largely lost in history. The idea of preserving buildings, documents and mementoes is a relatively recent activity. Our understanding of the past comes largely from essays and histories written by people who, far from recording an impartial view of what had transpired, inevitably wrote in line with the wishes of the monarch who paid them, or the church they served, or the particular politics, religion or philosophy they supported. E.H. Carr, the renowned English historian wrote a book titled "*What Is History?*" in 1961, which explores this issue. So there is little objective documentation about the early days of Freemasonry. Those few who were members and wrote of it had a vested interest in making it seem important, with a glittering history. Most contemporary writers who were not members, since they weren't in it, simply ignored it.

In the case of the Mark Degree, therefore, unless some important new document surfaces, it is next to impossible to determine whether the Ritual we practice now is a distillation of Rituals performed by the early stonemasons as they built the cathedrals and castles of Europe; or a complete fabrication from a later era arising from the fact that, due to rotting plaster falling off walls which exposed the bare stones beneath, people learned that the early stonemasons had put their mark or signature on their work, and incorporated this finding into the new Rituals they were inventing.

The first record of the mark being used in Freemasonry comes from June 8, 1600, when it is recorded the William Schaw, the 'Chief Maister of Masons', met with members of the Lodge of Edinburgh, Scotland, in the presence of the Laird of Auchinleck, who notarised the minutes of the meeting by appending his mark to them, as did the operatives; "That the day of ressanying (*receiving*) of the said fallow of Craft or Master be ord'lie buikit and his name and mark insert in the said buik (*book*)."

Since there were operative masons present as well, it is safe to conclude that, whether or not the act of selecting a mark was accompanied by a formal ceremony among operative masons, it was normal practice for minutes of meetings to be kept and marks to be registered in a Book of Marks, probably to be sure no two members of a Lodge selected the same one.

Sadly, since few records were kept during those formative years, the next clear evidence we have of speculative Masons having such a Degree is recorded in the minutes of Phoenix Royal Arch Chapter in Portsmouth, England on September 1, 1769, where it was recorded that: "The Pro. Grand Master bro't the Warrant of the Chapter and having lately rec'd the Mark, he made the Bre'n 'Mark Masons' and 'Mark Masters', and each chuse their 'Mark'."

It is worth noting that two Degrees are mentioned: Mark Mason and Mark Master. These two are still practiced in England, while in most of the rest of the world there is now only one Degree. It also demonstrates the very close connection between the Mark and the Royal Arch Degrees in those days. In the United States that close link has been maintained. However, in England at the Act of Union in 1813, when the Antients and Moderns came together to form the United Grand Lodge of England (UGLE), only the Holy Royal Arch survived as an 'officially sanctioned' Degree, albeit in that infamous attorney-speak phrase: "Antient Masonry consists of three degrees and no more, viz. those of the Entered Apprentice, the Fellow Craft, and the Master Mason including the Supreme Order of the Holy Royal Arch." But for the Mark Degree there was no such welcome, and from then until today it exists as a completely separate organization, unrecognized - but tolerated - by the UGLE.

In the United States the Mark Master Degree is more properly called the Honorary Degree of Mark Master. This is because a Mark Lodge cannot be held outside the confines of a Royal Arch Chapter, for it does not have an independent Warrant or Charter. Because of this the Degree is considered to be 'honorary'. It is worth noting that, in some States, Mark Lodges were independently chartered: Pennsylvania and New Jersey are two examples. The early transactions of the Grand Chapter of New York also show that a number of Mark Warrants were issued, and even Grand Chapter opened on the Mark Degree to transact certain business, and on the Royal Arch Degree to transact other affairs up till 1849, when among a series of proposed Amendments to the Constitution, Section 3 was amended to read: "No Dispensation or Warrant shall hereafter be granted for constituting Lodges of Most Excellent Masters, Past Masters, or Mark Master Masons, independent of a Chapter of Royal Arch Masons." The Amendment was adopted, and after that time Grand Chapter only met on the Royal Arch Degree.

KEY SYMBOLS IN THE MARK MASTER DEGREE

The name 'Mark' comes from the mark which laborers used to engrave upon their work to identify it as having been carved by them, and only them. This served a number of purposes. There can be no doubt that it was at least in part a matter of pride - rather like a painter signing his work with a flourish at the bottom right hand corner of the picture. Another reason was to show the Master who had carved each stone prior to their being added to the walls; and this would have required both an inspection of the work, to insure it was of high enough quality, and a bookkeeping system to record who had made which ashlars so that they could paid the right amount. Since stonemasons worked on hard stone and normally had only a chisel to work with, most marks were made up of straight lines, and only a few marks contain more intricate designs, such as arcs or circles.

Much is made of this symbolism in the Degree. In Genesis Adam was given the task naming the animals, and traditionally the act of naming something indicates ownership and control. Much care is taken in naming a child, since the name will represent that child throughout its life, and most parents are aware that names carry an attribute which they hope the child may exhibit. In the Royal Order of Scotland, a Masonic Order of Chivalry originating unsurprisingly in Scotland, each Knight is given an attribute, such as Patience or Accuracy, by which he is known in the Order, and which is added to his Certificate. Other Chivalric Orders also allow the Knight to select a new name or motto, which reflects the attribute he most wishes to emulate: even the pope changes his name upon election to identify with the saint or predecessor whose values he most admires. In the Mark Degree, by selecting one's own mark and symbolically putting it upon a stone, one is identifying with that stone, and that stone, now fit to be used in the building of the Temple, reflects the Spiritual Temple. We are all working upon ourselves, making ourselves individual smooth ashlars fit for use in that Temple: but we also realize that we are but one tiny part of the whole, and this reminds us that we are not only working towards our own reunion with God, but our duty is also to elevate all mankind to become one with us and with God.

Another important symbol in the Mark Master Degree is the Keystone. There are three main attributes of the keystone which separate it from the work undertaken in the first Three Degrees:

- "It is neither an oblong or a square", as the Overseers make mention;
- It incorporates an arc in its design;
- It is marked in a peculiar manner.

During the Blue Lodge Degrees we saw the progressive development of the Square and Compasses. We were told the Square represented earth, the microcosm; and the Compasses the heavens, the macrocosm. Man wields the Square, and in these degrees God wields the Compasses, as we see in the famous painting by William Blake, *The Ancient of Days*. By the Third Degree the Compasses had been liberated from the control of the square, and now sat on top, symbolizing the increasing importance of God in the Mason's words and actions.

Now in this 'fourth' Degree we see the Compasses put to work. The flared sides of the keystone can only be created by the action of the Compasses and the Square; and the arc of the top can only be designed by use of the Compasses alone. Man below, God above. Also, the New Name referred to in the Ritual is seen in initials upon the face of the keystone, but surrounded by a circle. If we remember the cartouches of ancient Egypt, which enclosed the names of the Gods and the Pharaohs, we understand that this New Name has been given to us by God, and as the scriptural passage says: "...and (I) will give him a white stone, and in the stone a new name written, which no man knoweth saving he that receiveth it" (Revelation 2:17).

In the Entered Apprentice Degree we were given a new name: *Caution*. In the Mark Degree that name is now superseded. The Apprentice Name is replaced with our True Name, our New Name.

Session 2
(Following the Virtual Past Master Degree)

INTRODUCTION

In this session the Candidate is given an overview of the Constitution since, like that of Grand Lodge, it underpins all the activities of Grand Chapter and regulates the smooth running of all Chapters in the jurisdiction.

At this stage the particular Charities supported by the Grand Chapter are introduced, and the importance of demonstrating those commitments to charity made when one first became a Mason are underlined.

Then the history of the Virtual Past Master Degree explains why this Degree is included in the Capitular series of Degrees, and why this is no longer required in some other jurisdictions.

SECOND SESSION SUBJECTS

1. The Constitution
2. The Royal Arch Charities
3. Why a Past Master Degree?
4. The Virtual Past Master Degree

THE CONSTITUTION

A Constitution is defined as "a body of fundamental principles or established precedents according to which a state or other organization is acknowledged to be governed."

The importance of Constitutions to Freemasons can be seen from the fact that Bro. James Anderson printed the first Constitutions in 1723, the same year that the Premier Grand Lodge of England appointed their first Grand Secretary. Another indication of their importance is found in the fact that a reprint of these Constitutions was the first Masonic book printed in America, by Benjamin Franklin, in Philadelphia in 1734.

Similarly, the Antients' Grand Lodge was founded in 1751 and by 1756 Laurence Dermott had compiled *Ahiman Rezon*, the Constitutions of the Antients.

This first book contains a number of different parts in addition to the Constitutions themselves. It begins with a dedication to the Grand Master, Lord Montagu, which is followed by an inventive history tracing Masonic roots from Adam to King George I. There is an extended treatment of the Seven Ancient Wonders of the World, emphasizing their architectural and geometric foundation, as well as several songs. As a book which contains history, laws, songs and explanatory passages, there is a clear link with the Holy Bible, which itself is a compilation of similar threads.

Of course the most important parts of the *Constitutions* are the *General Regulations* and the *Charges of a Free-mason*. The *Charges* develop the idea of how a Mason should conduct himself throughout his life, including his duties to his country, his fellow man and his Brethren; and the *General Regulations* govern the activities of the Grand Lodge and Lodge Officers.

The Constitution of New York was originally written in the 1770s while the Grand Lodge was still under the jurisdiction of the Provincial Grand Lodge reporting to the Premier Grand Lodge of England. In 1781 it briefly changed its allegiance to the Antients' Grand Lodge, before finally declaring independence to form a sovereign Grand Lodge. Since then the Constitutions have expanded from a relatively thin book, which was still only 143 pages in 1877, to the 700 pages it now contains. Most of the increase does not reflect and expansion of powers or duties: rather it reflects an ever-increasing body of rulings, opinions and interpretations of the Statutes, Rules and Regulations arising from Masonic trials.

Now we have a general understanding of Constitutions, we are in a position to look at the Constitutions of the Grand Chapter of the State of New York, Royal Arch Masons.

A Committee to draft a set of Constitutions was approved at the Annual Communication on Feb 2 1802. After three years' work, the first Constitutions of the Grand Chapter of New York were adopted on February 7, 1805. Prior to this the Grand Chapters worked under the Constitution of the General Grand Chapter. Thomas Smith Webb, who we met earlier, drafted these Constitutions. However, it was quickly determined that the Grand Chapter should be sovereign, and General Grand Chapter adopted an advisory role. So seven years after the Grand Chapter of New York was founded it approved its first Constitution.

The Constitution of the State of New York is actually quite compact, being only around twelve pages long; and even in 2014 it is only around 46 pages long, excluding appendices and index. The actual content of the Constitution has changed little over the years. While it contains the composition and duties of Grand Chapter and its subordinate Chapters, most of the regulations on discipline refer to Chapter only, since it has long been an accepted fact that, if a Companion violates any of its rules, these are the same rules as those of Grand Lodge, and since Grand Lodge is the senior Masonic body in the State, it is appropriate that its Proctor prosecute the miscreant rather than maintain a parallel system in Grand Chapter.

The main Sections of the Constitution are as follows:

Article I:	The Grand Chapter	-	Name, authority, members, title, votes, duties of Grand Line Officers.
Article II:	The Grand Chapter Funds & Foundations	-	Funds and Charities
Article III:	Subordinate Chapters	-	Organization, Officers, Degrees, Annual Returns, Duties of Officers
Article IV:	Candidates	-	Jurisdiction, Qualifications, Petitions, Balloting
Article V:	Conferring Degrees	-	Standard Work, Fees, Order of conferral
Article VI:	Discipline	-	Charges and trials, Appeals, Restoration

Article VII:	Amendments & Resolutions	- Process for proposing amendments to the Constitution

Perhaps the most important Section of all is that which covers unanticipated issues. Unlike the Grand Lodge Constitutions which his constantly growing, Section 703 simply states: "In the event that there is any dispute as to the meaning of this Constitution or in the event that there are any omissions therefrom, the Constitutions of the Grand Lodge of Free and Accepted Masons of the State of New York shall apply."

THE ROYAL ARCH CHARITIES

A fundamental activity of all Masonic bodies is the practice of charity, and the Grand Chapter of New York is no exception. It is proud to sponsor three particular charities. The good news is, over the years our Companions have been extremely generous. Indeed, in the past five years annual contributions to our charities have been around $60,000 a year! Our charitable funds total several million dollars.

In New York State our three Charity Programs are:

- The Royal Arch Scholarship Fund
- The Medical Research Foundation
- The Medical Relief Fund

All of the Charities work in two directions - in collecting money from the Companions to put to good use; and distributing that money and the interest being earned on the funds to worthy Companions and their families.

Each Capitular District has three local officers representing the Grand Chapter. The District Deputy Grand High Priest represents the Grand High Priest, and it is his duty to supervise the District, make an official visit to each Chapter during his year, review the books and records, and run the District on behalf of the Grand High Priest. The Assistant Grand Lecturer is responsible for helping Chapters to put on good rituals, to make sure they certify, to arrange the Grand Lecturer's Convention in the District, and to take primary responsibility for running the many courses available to the Companions. The third - and equally important - is the Charity Chairman. It is his responsibility to try to maximize the charitable contributions of his District. He liaises with the Charity Committee, runs fund-raisers, such as a Capitular Table Lodge or a Scholarship Fund-raising Dinner in his District, and any other events to raise money for the Charities, sells the Scholarship seals (see below) and is the first point person for those seeking charitable relief from our funds.

The **Royal Arch Scholarship Fund** provides scholarships of $500 and $1,000 to children, grandchildren and families of Royal Arch Companions. This includes Companions or their wives who are going back to school. Money is raised through the sale of the Royal Arch seals, and through the twice yearly fundraising activities of the Charities Committee. The pages of Royal Arch seals were designed by one of our talented Brazilian Companions a few years ago. They cost a mere $2 a sheet, and every cent goes directly to scholarships. The seals can be used on any letter and make a colorful addition to envelopes! Those seeking a scholarship are asked to complete an Application Form between January 1st and April 1st. They are awarded on scholastic achievement, character and financial need. The forms need to be sent the Charity Chairman in a timely manner, and the Committee determines how the scholarships are awarded. To avoid any possibility of favoritism, the applications are assigned numbers so the Committee has no idea who they are considering. The scholarships are presented in July, at several locations across the State in tandem with Grand Lodge.

The **Medical Research Foundation** supports charitable activities associated with the Medical Research Facility in Utica and other medical facilities as well. The Grand Lodge maintains an extensive campus in Utica, with buildings dedicated to Grand Lodge and the various Concordant Bodies, as well as the Thompkins Chapel, a synagogue, a conference hall and stage. It also maintains a Retirement Home, a managed Senior Healthcare Facility, a Hospital and a state-of-the-art Research Center. The Grand Chapter paid for the construction of a two floor Royal Arch Medical Research Wing, and over the past decades has donated over a million dollars to medical research.

The **Medical Relief Fund** (formerly the *Diseases of the Lungs Fund*) was initially set up to help those suffering from the effects of illnesses associated with such professions as mining and trades involving the use of asbestos. However, since those professions are no longer prominent in our State, the focus on this fund has expanded to any diseases - including cancer - which affect the lungs. The size of the funds means that we no longer need to raise money for it. However, it is available to any Companion or direct family who is in financial need due to the costs associated with such a disease, including transportation to and from hospital, CPAP equipment, nursing visits and similar needs. A couple of years ago this charity funded the installation of an oxygen system to all the beds in the hospital facility. Anyone who knows of a Companion suffering from any disease affecting the lungs is encouraged to bring it to the attention of their High Priest, who can find the necessary forms on our website and being the process to bring a measure of financial relief to him and his family. It is expected that this fund will further broaden its scope over time, subject to legal restrictions on use.

Companions should receive communications from the Chairman of the Charities Committee twice a year, and also District activities being organized by the District Charity Chairman; and of course all Companions are encouraged to support these worthy activities. Donations may be earmarked for a specific charity, or given to the GHP Discretionary Fund, which he will assign to each charity according to its immediate need.

All Companions are also encouraged to visit the website at ny-royal-arch.org, where there is a shop offering all manner of branded attire, a proportion of the revenue going to our charities.

Finally, the Zerubbabel Society was introduced a few years ago, and has proved so popular it has been taken up by a number of other States. A Companion commits to donating $1,000 to charity, at a rate of $100 a year (or more if he can afford it). In return he is presented with an attractive jewel which he may wear at all Royal Arch functions; and a pin with a red ruby-like jewel, which is replaced by a diamond-like jewel once he has completed his pledge. This alone has been responsible for locking in a charity cash flow of several hundred thousand dollars over the coming years!

The Grand Chapter is proud to support such worthy causes, from encouraging our children toward further education, through supporting research to relieve significant medical conditions, to caring for our older Companions when respiratory functions become an issue.

WHY A PAST MASTER DEGREE?

The requirement for being a Past Master of a regular Lodge prior to receiving the Holy Royal Arch was a stated requirement from the earliest times of Freemasonry. In *Ahiman Rezon*, Laurence Dermott says:

"Having inserted this prayer, and mentioned that part of Masonry commonly called the Royal Arch (which I firmly believe to be the root-heart and marrow of masonry) I cannot forbear giving a hint of a certain evil designer, who has made a trade thereof for some time past, and has drawn in a number of worthy, honest men, and made them believe that he and his associates truly taught them all and every part of the abovementioned branch of masonry... This is the case of all those who think themselves Royal Arch Masons, without passing the chair in regular form, according to the ancient customs of the craft."

He goes on to quote Bro. and Doctor Assigny, who in 1744 wrote: "And as it is an organized body of men who have passed the chair, and given undeniable proofs of their skill in architecture, it cannot be treated with too much reverence; and more especially since the characters of the present members of that particular lodge are untainted, and their behaviour judicious and unexceptional: so that there cannot be the least hinge to hang a doubt on, but that they are most excellent masons."

The almost complete absence of the Royal Arch Degree in the Premier Grand Lodge established in 1717 is strange. It is unlikely that the Royal Arch sprang fully-formed from nowhere to become the centerpiece of the Antient rituals. It was certainly known, and we find several references to it in the records of the Premier Grand Lodge. However, it never played an important role until the Act of Union in 1813, when it was finally admitted as one of the Degrees overseen by the United Grand Lodge, albeit not directly, but by a Supreme Grand Chapter. Indeed, it is often argued that the desire to restore the Royal Arch Degree was one of the main reasons the Antients split from the Moderns in the first place. Some modern scholars suggest an alternative: that the Antients were not a schismatic group from the Premier Grand Lodge, but rather a completely independent group, possibly Masons of Irish descent, who formed a new Grand Lodge following the practices of their 'mother' Grand Lodge - that of Ireland. If this is the case, then the immediate appearance of the Royal Arch, which was a feature of Irish Masonry, would have a logical explanation.

In both cases possession of the 'chair' Degree was considered essential. So the Degree was not freely available to the 'rank and file', but only to those who had presided over a Lodge and were now Past Masters. Given the small number of Lodges in the early days it can readily be seen that the survival of the Royal Arch was clearly going to be a problem with so few people eligible to join, and it was not long before we see the emergence of an exercise called 'passing the chair', in which several Master Masons would be seated in the oriental throne for a moment, entrusted with the words of a Past Master, and thereby become eligible to receive the Royal Arch Degree.

At the Act of Union it was decided that a simpler method would be to allow all Master Masons to join (especially since the Mark Master Degree was no longer a requirement, since that Degree was excluded from those recognized by the United Grand Lodge). All Master Masons of one year's standing could now join a Chapter. Most Lodges had a Chapter associated with them: it bore the same name and number as the Lodge. Later the time requirement was dropped to one month. However, a person who had been initiated, and now called a 'Companion', was not allowed to hold any of the three most senior offices unless they had sat as a Master of a Blue Lodge. This solution worked well for the English and other jurisdictions, since, if one or two Lodges 'fed' a Chapter, and those Lodges had a new Master each year, there would always be a new candidate for the three principal chairs.

Of course, the Act of Union had no effect in the United States, since they had parted company with England in the Revolutionary War, and the Grand Lodges had declared independence from the Ancients or Moderns decades before 1813. Because of this, the new approach of opening up the Royal Arch to all Master Masons was not adopted here, and to this day the Degree of Virtual Past Master is practiced as a requirement for any Brother to be received into a Chapter.

THE VIRTUAL PAST MASTER DEGREE

It may seem unusual to New York Masons that only a few American Grand Lodges require a Master Mason to have gone through the Degree of Past Master prior to assuming the office of Worshipful Master. In fact, not very many Grand Lodges require it. The reason New York requires it is probably an indication of the pride with which it traces its origins as an Antient Provincial Grand Lodge. In the early days of the York Rite, a Master who had been through the Ceremony was not required to take the Virtual Past Master Degree. It has been argued that this demonstrates the two rituals were identical, but there is an argument why this might have not been the case.

Masonic membership is normally highly regarded, and any member of a particular Order - especially an invitational one - would not lightly share it with a non-member. Any European Mason will tell you how highly prized the Installation Ceremony is held: in England, for example, the Installation of the new Master is the highlight of the year. Also, every Masonic body has its own Ritual of Installation, from the Mark Lodge to the Scottish Rite Chapter; and each has its own unique *Secrets of the Chair*, as they are sometimes called. It therefore seems highly unlikely that those who had earned the approbation of their Brethren, been elected to preside over them and served in this arduous role for a year (or six months in former times, from one St. John's Day to the next), would freely give those secrets to another for simply sitting in a chair for a couple of minutes! A recent Order to these shores, the Operatives, required a member to have presided over a Mark Lodge to reach a certain Degree. Since the Mark Degree is 'honorary' in the United States, rather than waive this requirement, the early pioneers of this Order had to travel to Canada - where Mark Lodges are run independently to the York Rite - on a regular basis, go through the offices and be elected Master, in order to receive the Secrets of the Chair, thereby becoming eligible to attain the next Grade in the Operatives in the United States! It is therefore probable that either the

Word, or Grip, or both were slightly different in the early days. Another indication might be the choice of biblical passage: Ecclesiastes XII is used in the New York Ritual, as it is in the Master Mason Degree. But in the English version - and perhaps in earlier ceremonies in the former colonies, I Kings X is used, which refers to the arrival of the Queen of Sheba to admire the newly-built Temple.

This way a Lodge of Past Masters could immediately tell if someone seeking entrance was an Actual Past Master (as those who had served in that position in a regular Lodge were called), or a Virtual Past Master (as those who had passed the chair in the York Rite were later called), who would then be excluded, since they were not entitled to that privilege.

Although the first use of the word 'virtual' is found in minutes dated January 1, 1800, it is believed that the phrase 'passed the chair' referred to both Actual and Virtual Past Masters prior to that time. For example, from a minute in 1792 in Ireland, two Brethren "pass'd the Chair preparatory to Receiving the Higher Degrees."

It is curious to note that, while no end of words have been written explaining *how* the Part Master Degree (Actual or Virtual) was considered an essential prerequisite to receiving the Holy Royal Arch Degree, little to nothing has been written about *why* this was the case!

Two possibilities point to a symbolic or historical reason.

Symbolically speaking, in going through the Past Master Degree the Mason is finally identified with King Solomon, having played the part of one of his workmen through the preceding Degrees. Perhaps this was seen as necessary to identify with the role played by Zerubbabel as his alleged descendant in the Royal Arch Degree, as a ruler in the Craft. Historically speaking, it may be that the Royal Arch Degree was closely associated with the status of Past Master in the past. Perhaps at one time it *was* the Past Master Degree? Either theory is possible; or there may be another completely different reason not previously considered. Remember that, even in the English system, where any Mason may join, only an Actual Past Master may preside.

The present day ceremony follows closely that of the Blue Lodge, combining the Investiture and Installation Ceremonies. There is an election, followed by the same Obligation as that of Master-elect, after which the Grip and Word are communicated. The ceremony then closely follows the Installation, but ends with a caution in the Address: that "Your receiving this degree confers upon you no official rank outside of the Chapter. The honors and peculiar privileges belonging to the Chair of Symbolic Lodges are confined exclusively to those who have been 'duly elected to preside over and govern' such Lodges."

It is curious to note that this Degree specifies that every Candidate must go through all the steps of the Degree: there is no exemplar. All must be 'elected', take the Obligation, be invested, covered, and 'pursue and perform some act of authority while holding the gavel.' If this were merely symbolic, there would be little reason to insist on this. What is does indicate, perhaps, is a belief that *participation* in the ceremony of Installation transmits some kind of quality which mere *observation* does not.

Session 3
(Following the Most Excellent Master Degree)

INTRODUCTION

In this session the Candidate reviews the Officers in the three Degrees leading up to the Holy Royal Arch, and compares them to those in the Blue Lodge. These Officers indicate a common ancestry for these Degrees.

The General Grand Chapter is the body which stands over the jurisdictions which follow the American Rite. However, unlike Grand Encampment, the body which administers the Grand Commanderies of Knights Templar, it is an advisory organization rather than an executive one. This body has strong links to New York, and some of the greatest Masons from our State have a close connection with General Grand Chapter.

The Degree is then examined and some of the key symbols and messages are considered in greater depth. This is a 'pivot' Degree in that it leads from the conclusion of the Fraternal Degrees to a new Order whose members are called Companions, who meet in a Chapter rather than a Lodge. The importance of this is considered and a first hint at the important esoteric implications of this new status is given.

THIRD SESSION SUBJECTS

1. The Officers of the Royal Arch Lodges
2. General Grand Chapter
3. The Most Excellent Master Degree
4. Key Symbols in the Most Excellent Master Degree

THE OFFICERS OF THE ROYAL ARCH LODGES

By now it should be apparent that the Degrees do not follow a chronological sequence. The Blue Lodge Degree can perhaps be accepted as following in chronological order - though there is no particular reason to place the Entered Apprentice and Fellowcraft Degrees prior to the Master Mason Degree. Indeed, one might argue that the Temple must have been completed or nearly completed for there to be a second floor to access by means of the winding staircase. Still, it becomes immediately apparent that, in the Mark Master Degree, we have gone back to a time immediately prior to the death of Hiram Abif, since the story revolves around the discovery of a stone which had been created by him. Only later is his absence noticed. The Virtual Past Master is in a way timeless, in that it doesn't fit into any particular point in the story. Finally, the Most Excellent Master Degree, through which you have just passed, tells the story of the Dedication of the Temple. Hiram Abif was slain just prior to the completion of the Temple in the eighth month, and the Temple was dedicated in the seventh month of the following year. His death is fondly recalled, not in terms of the great personal pain felt by King Solomon in the Third Degree Drama, but now rather as a strong yet healing memory, and an expression of regret for his absence.

If we look at the Officers in the Mark Master Degree, the first thing we notice is that the presiding Officer is called the 'Right Worshipful Master'. Nowadays we are used to this title indicating a senior position in Grand Lodge, perhaps a District Staff Officer or District Deputy Grand Master, or an Officer in Grand Lodge up to and including the Deputy Grand Master. In some jurisdictions even the Grand Master keeps the title Right Worshipful.

Why the promotion? There are two possible reasons. Firstly, it may be to emphasize the fact that the Presiding Officer represents King Solomon throughout the Degree, and therefore dignifies him with the title of a Grand Master. Secondly, it may indicate the origin of the Mark Degree, as practiced here, as having originated in Scotland. In that jurisdiction all Lodges (as well as Royal Arch Chapters) are authorized to confer the Mark Degree; and the Master of a Lodge is traditionally called 'Right Worshipful Master'. Given the Scottish and Northern English Masons (who may have attended such meetings across the border) who settled in the colonies, as well as the Scottish military forces who were stationed here, this is a likely source of the title.

Eight Officers are required for the Mark Master Degree. In addition to the usual five Officers of Master, Wardens and Deacons, we find three Overseers. Their role is interesting. Before, the learner was paid in corn, wine and oil. Now the Mark Mason is paid money (*specie*, as it is sometimes called in the ritual). Here the Candidate is going to offer up his own work for inspection by the Overseers and receive payment from the Senior Warden. What is interesting is the fact that, although the Junior and Senior Overseers do not recognize the object presented to them, they recognize its intrinsic beauty and allow it to pass on. There is an allegory of spiritual truth here: although these men are not yet sufficiently spiritually aware to recognize the true value of the keystone, still they perceive there is something special about it, which allows them to recognize that it is worthy of preservation.

What are we to make of the number eight? Eight is considered to be a perfect number, the product of 2 x 2 x 2, or a perfect cube. This, after all, is the goal of the Master Mason, to carve a perfect ashlar.

Did you spot the error in the Degree, one which has nevertheless been perpetuated since the Ritual was first codified by Thomas Smith Webb? In the Second Part of the Degree there is a Junior Warden, who even challenges the Candidates on their way to take the Obligation of a Mark Master Mason. And yet the Degree is predicated upon the fact that Hiram Abif, who the Junior Warden represents, was slain after he had completed the keystone and prior to its discovery! Indeed, it is best if the Junior Warden vacates his station some time during the conferral of the grips and words, since immediately after this a trestleboard is set up by his Station to bear the design of the Keystone. The conversation which follows would make no sense at all if the Junior Warden, representing Hiram Abif, was still sitting in the South.

The Virtual Past Master Degree uses five Officers, the same as a Blue Lodge. Although the Junior Warden has no part he is definitely present, since he is referred to in the rubric when the Obligation is taken. The Past Master Degree takes place at no particular time, so at first glance there would seem to be no reason why the Junior Warden, representing Hiram Abif, should not be present. Indeed, none of the Blue Lodge Degrees indicate that King Solomon, Hiram King of Tyre and Hiram Abif were not making Master Masons prior to his death. Indeed, the implication that the three Overseers are Master Masons suggests they did. After all, a Master Mason is not a Grand Master, and we are only told that they could *no longer* make Master Masons when Hiram Abif was murdered.

The odd fact about the Officers in the Virtual Past Master Degree is that the Senior and Junior Wardens are not referred to as Worshipful Senior and Junior Wardens, but as Brothers. In the Investiture Ceremony for a Master-elect, only Past Masters are present at the conferral of the Secrets of the Chair. In the English Ritual of Installation, all the Officers' chairs are filled by Past Masters. The Officers are called Worshipful Installing Officer, Worshipful Senior Warden, Worshipful Junior Warden, Worshipful Senior Deacon and Worshipful Junior Deacon. So it is noteworthy that, despite the fact that they are referred to as Brother (for example: "Brother Marshall, introduce the Candidates") in this Ceremony, all the Officers are present when the Secrets are communicated. The reason, of course, is that all the Officers are Virtual Past Masters. However, it does make the Officers' titles used a little strange.

Finally, in the Most Excellent Master Degree we find four Officers. The Junior Warden is finally no longer present, and we are left with the Master, Senior Warden, Senior and Junior Deacons. It is interesting to consider the numbers used in each of the Degrees. We are told that "three rule a Lodge, five hold a Lodge and seven make it perfect." This is reflected in the idea that seven are needed for an Entered Apprentice Lodge, five for a Fellowcraft Lodge and three for a Master Masons Lodge. This also implies that a 'perfect' Lodge is composed of three Master Masons, two Fellowcraft and two Entered Apprentices.

In our Degrees we have gone from 7 (EA), 5 (FC), 3 (MM), 8 (MMM), 5 (VPM) and now 4 (MEM). Every number has a symbolic meaning. The number four has often been associated with Earth, since the numbers can represent the four ancient elements of Earth, Air, Fire and Water. The Greek classical elements are often supplemented by the addition of a fifth element: Spirit. This symbolism was used heavily by the Alchemists, who believed that by finding a way to vivify elements, usually base metals, they could raise the quality of that metal, or bring life to the inanimate object, thereby creating a 'living stone', the so-called Stone of the Philosophers. They used the early verses of Genesis as their inspiration: as God breathed spirit into clay to create Adam, so they could infuse life into earthly elements.

Here the four human representatives of the elements are indeed joined by the fifth element of spirit, in the symbol of the Ark of the Covenant, which unites those present in the living Temple. For as we are told in the Scriptures, the Temple was but a building until the Ark was safely seated, and God dwelled within.

It is worth bearing in mind, through this example, that our Rituals are so full of symbolism, that every object, every nuance, every line and, as we have seen, even the numbers of Officers can carry an important teaching for us.

GENERAL GRAND CHAPTER

It is interesting to note that, in the early days of Freemasonry in this country, there was a movement to create a General Grand Lodge body to sit with authority over all the Grand Lodges in the United States. Indeed, at one time it was contemplated that George Washington should be the first 'General Grand Master'! History shows us that this idea did not gain wide support, and each State is sovereign and independent regarding Blue Lodge Masonry. Indeed, in most States the Grand Master also decides which of the other Masonic bodies, from major ones like the Scottish Rite and Royal Arch, to the smaller and newer ones, such as the Commemorative Order of St. Thomas of Acon and the Operatives, may function in his State.

In other cases the United States may find itself as a Province of Orders originating in other countries, as in the case of the two above mentioned Orders; and in other cases where the Rite was invented here, the Sovereign Body may be located in the United States. An example of this is the York Rite Sovereign College, based in Detroit, which administers the York Rite Colleges across the country. These bodies, while requiring permission of the Grand Master of their State in order to exist, nonetheless report directly to their own Sovereign Body. Another example would be the Scottish Rite, which has two Sovereign Administrative Organizations, the Northern and the Southern Masonic Jurisdictions, based in Lexington, MA and Washington, DC respectively.

In the case of the York Rite, which is really composed of four bodies - Lodge, Chapter, Council and Commandery - each has its own State Grand Body, and also a National Body which, figuratively speaking at least, oversees the activities of the State Grand Bodies.

It should come as no surprise that these National Bodies were thought up, designed and implemented by that intrepid leader of North Eastern Freemasonry - Thomas Smith Webb.

Initially these bodies were conceived as wielding authority over the subordinate bodies - indeed, in the earliest days the head of a State Royal Arch Body was called the Deputy Grand High Priest, and only the General Grand High Priest had the absolute title of 'Grand High Priest'. That sovereignty continues today in the Grand Encampment of Knights Templar, in which the Grand Master has absolute authority over of the Grand Commanderies. Nevertheless, like all Grand Bodies, he is accountable to his Grand Encampment, and his actions are approved or otherwise at a Triennial meeting, just as a Grand Master's activities are approved in plenary session at the Annual Communication.

When General Grand Chapter was originally organized on October 24, 1797, initially by Chapters representing Massachusetts, Rhode Island and New York, it was intended to have similar authority over the subordinate Grand Chapters. However, very early on in its history it gave up claims to such power and instead became an advisory body; while the individual Grand Chapters, now run by Grand High Priests, were sovereign.

Over the years the General Grand Chapter has made itself invaluable to Royal Arch Masonry through its many activities, and now counts the Companions of most of the United States, as well as many other countries around the world, particularly in Latin America and the former Communist bloc; and more recently in Africa, among its members. When a country wishes to introduce Royal

Arch Masonry, it usually approaches General Grand Chapter first. This body provides the support and education necessary to establish the first Chapter in that country. Once that country has established three Chapters certified by General Grand Chapter as being fully functional and independent, a Grand Chapter is established, and that country now becomes sovereign and independent of General Grand Chapter, but a voting member of it.

Every three years the General Grand Chapter, in conjunction with the General Grand Cryptic Council, holds a Triennial, at which a new General Grand High Priest, General Grand King and General Grand Scribe are elected. All terms last three years until the next Triennial. In reality only the General Grand Scribe is contested, since the other two offices normally move up to the next position. General Grand Chapter has a Grand Line similar to Grand Chapters. In addition a number of Deputy General Grand High Priests are appointed to represent the General Grand High Priest in regions of the United States and the world. Finally each Country, Province (several Canadian Provinces are also members) or State has an Ambassador, who functions like a Grand Representative, representing General Grand Chapter to that State.

In addition to its role in helping new territories to establish Chapters and eventually Grand Chapters, the General Grand Chapter acts as a clearing house for education, historical records and ideas for the betterment of its Companions. It also involves itself in charity work, particularly the Royal Arch Research Assistance ('RARA') which provides funds to support research into autism and CAPD. The organization also circulates an informative quarterly magazine, the Royal Arch Mason, to all Companions of Grand Chapter who contribute; and Companions may also subscribe on-line to an electronic newsletter, the International Royal Arch Mason News. Finally, the General Grand Chapter offers a number of awards to recognize excellence in service to Capitular Masonry. on completing a rigorous series of ritual assignments, a Companion is entitled to receive the Ritual Jewel. There are also Bronze, Silver and Gold Medals for exemplary service, and even a Sweetheart Award for long-suffering - and active - wives!

Like the Grand Masters' Conference, the Triennial is an ideal setting for an exchange of ideas between senior Companions from around the world, and its sessions are open to all Companions - though voting is restricted to the Elected Line from each State, including the Grand Council and Grand High Priests who have previously served.

THE MOST EXCELLENT MASTER DEGREE

The version of the Most Excellent Master Degree practiced in the United States was certainly authored by Thomas Smith Webb, and is considered a masterpiece of symbolism and biblical integration and interpretation. It is arguably one of the most satisfying of all the Masonic Degrees. Webb did not invent the Ritual - indeed there is much speculation on whether an early Degree existed which integrated both the discovery of the Keystone (in what is now the Mark Master Degree) and its placement in the Temple - but he certainly took it to a sublime place.

This Degree culminates everything which took place before, and is a logical conclusion to the building of the Temple and the untimely death of Hiram Abif prior to its completion. In this Degree the Temple is finally completed, and the solemn ceremonies of its Dedication enacted.

Following the Obligation, in which the Candidate is reminded that, as a fully informed Mason, he will dispense Masonic light to his "less informed Brethren." It should also be noted that the Grip in this Degree is similar to the Sign in the Past Master Degree, in that is shares the characteristic of being a summary of the preceding ones. Finally, it is interesting to note that, of all the Degrees, this is the only one in which the Pass Word and True Word are given at their correct times: the Pass Word to gain admittance and the True Word given after taking the Obligation. In most other jurisdictions this is how the two words are used in every Degree: the pass word given as a reward for memorizing the catechism of the preceding Degree and reciting it in Open Lodge as a means to satisfy the Sentinel once the Lodge is open on the next Degree; and the True Word given once the Candidate is Obligated not to reveal the secrets of that Degree.

This ends the First Section. The Second Section is a reenactment of the Completion and Dedication. The senior Officers take on their *personae* as King Solomon and Hiram King of Tyre, and costumes are often worn.

The Dedication Ode bears testimony to Thomas Smith Webb's love of music, and is a suitable modern day equivalent to the Psalms of David, which were no doubt sung on that original joyous event, in honor of God and King Solomon's father, who had conceived - but was not permitted to build - the Temple. The Keystone is seated and, since labor has now officially ended, the Workmen are called upon to remove their aprons. Although this is a play rather than formal ritual, it is an odd feeling indeed to remove one's apron in a Lodge Room setting. At this point the Candidate is 'accepted and received' Most Excellent Master. For the first time he is greeted as an equal by the two monarchs.

The Second Section is also the first time all the key paraphernalia of the Temple is seen. Despite the fact that most Degrees have taken place at least partly within the Temple, before this moment we have not seen the Menorah, the Table of Shewbread, the Altar of Incense and the Ark of the Covenant. As an aside one might remember that one hundred or more years ago, anyone entering the room and seeing these object would immediately recall the story of the Temple's Completion since the Bible would have been read many times. Sadly this is no longer the case, and it is probable that most Candidates, on seeing these objects, would either have only a dim understanding of their origin, or no idea at all of what they represent. It is worth opening the Holy Bible presented to us during one of the Blue Lodge Degrees and reading the story of the Completion and Dedication of the Temple in detail, to make that 'daily advance in Masonic knowledge' we so earnestly promise to do!

Most of the Dedication section is taken directly from the Scriptures. The only part which is not in the Bible is the regret expressed by the two monarchs that Hiram Abif is not present to join in the celebrations. In this Degree we have two 'miracles which hark back to those early times when simple peasants would stand outside the cathedral doors watching reenactments by the Guilds of the Biblical stories. In this case a mysterious light, the Shekinah, appears either above of glowing behind the Ark; and in a wonderful display of pyrotechnics rarely allowed in Lodge Rooms nowadays, fire descends from the heavens to light the Altar of Incense. This is indeed a fitting climax to this highly visual Ritual. The beautiful prayers of Solomon over his people and his supplication to God are reproduced in their entirety, before the two kings repeat Psalm 122: "I was glad when they said unto me, Let us go into the House of the Lord."

Finally we are told: "We are reminded that we should also dedicate our spiritual building, that Temple which we have been erecting within ourselves to the service of the same Supreme Being... And that in the process of time, even at the best, the decay of ages will crumble our magnificent temple into dust. Yet we are persuaded that, if we have erected the temple of our inner life by Square, Plumb line, and Rule, its foundation shall never fail, and its fabrics shall never crumble or decay."

And those lines set the scene for the Holy Royal Arch Degree. *Adhuc Stat*!

KEY SYMBOLS IN THE MOST EXCELLENT MASTER DEGREE

It was mentioned earlier that numbers play an important symbolic role in Freemasonry. This is also true of the Holy Bible, where numbers are often used to convey a particular meaning. For example, the number '40' was often used to depict a time or trial or testing. We see this in Noah's Flood, where the waters remained upon the earth for 40 days (Genesis 7:4); or the 40 days that Moses was on the mountain with God (Exodus 24:18); and again the number of years the Israelites wandered in the desert (Numbers 14:33-34); David and Solomon both reigned 40 years (1 Kings 2:11; 1 Kings 11:42); Jesus was tempted 40 days in the wilderness (Mark 1:13). We have also seen that the number '4' represents earth, or earthly things - from temptation (Jesus) to failing tests (David's lust and Solomon's turning from his Faith).

Similarly, Jewish scholars, Commentators and Cabbalists (esoteric scholars) have made much of the similarities in the descriptions of the creation of the world and of Adam and the creation of the Temple, including the time taken to complete both. We read God created the Universe in six days, and rested on the seventh. We are also told Solomon created the Temple in six years and it was almost a year before it was dedicated, in the seventh year. In both cases an act of God brought life into the shell: God's breath into Adam and the descent of the Shekinah into the Temple. This led many to see a link between man (Adam) and the Temple. This is one reason some Masonic scholars believe the Temple of Solomon was a carefully chosen vehicle through which to teach lessons of morality, truth and spirituality.

As a hint of further symbolic significance, the Menorah holds seven lights or candles; and the Table of Shewbread twelve loaves. Again we see the numbers 7 and 12. The lights are a worthy symbol of the heavens and the seven then known planets, as well as the cycle of the week, and a sign of the perfection of God's Creation. The bread, earthly sustenance of man, represents the twelve months by which the cycle of our lives is governed, reflected in the heavens by the zodiac. These two numbers signify the eternal and the temporal, heaven and earth, the creative actions of God and of man.

From this viewpoint the completion and Dedication of the Temple becomes a powerful allegory.

The first part of the ceremony proceeds much like the previous ones, but without a preamble as in the Mark Degree. Note that the Candidate is tried this time by the Keystone - the first time a piece of work rather than an implement is used to try him. Instead of being symbolically worked upon, by square, compasses or chisel, he is now identified with the Keystone itself.

The Candidate then performs six circuits about the Lodge, the number 6 linking that journey with the days of Creation, or the year it took to build the Temple. And at the end of that circular journey, implying the use of the Compasses of Creation, we note a significant development in the manner in which the Brethren stand around the Candidate kneeling at the altar. In the Blue Lodge they formed a rectangular symbolic temple. In the Mark and Past Master Degrees they formed two parallel lines extending East and West. Now for the first time they form a circle about the Candidate. The angles have finally become the line without angles, the sign of perfection, or excellence.

As one parting thought on the symbolism of this Degree, let us remember that once the Keystone is positioned and the Temple is completed, the Temple is now perfect. There is no further need to labor upon it. Therefore the aprons are removed. Man is viewed as a being who was initially perfect, indeed the very image of God. However, through his own transgression he fell from a state of grace, and since then has been trying to retrace his steps towards God. In our tradition the symbols of the Fall was the putting on of clothes, or aprons as it is described in some translations of the Bible. It is for this reason that Anderson in his Constitutions claimed that Adam was the first Mason! But now the Temple is perfected, and by analogy we are symbolically perfected. We no longer need to wear the external symbol of our pupilage. We take our aprons off. We are reunited with God, and He shows his approbation in the Shekinah, the spirit of His presence among us.

Session 4
(Following the Holy Royal Arch Degree)

INTRODUCTION

The Grand Chapter of Royal Arch Masons as the Sovereign Body is now reviewed, and the key roles compared and contrasted to Grand Lodge. The functions and duties of Grand Chapter towards its members is considered.

The idea of Blue versus Red Masonry is considered, and the history of the colors purple and white in the historical context of Freemasonry as well.

The context of the Royal Arch is considered, and also some theories about the origins of the Royal Arch, explaining that this is an integral part of Freemasonry. This is an important point which emphasizes the fact that the True Word of Master Mason is not a modern addition, but goes back to the earliest days of Freemasonry, and therefore the True Word was probably the original word.

FOURTH SESSION SUBJECTS

1. Grand Chapter Organization
2. Blue and Red Masonry
3. Context of The Holy Royal Arch Degree
4. Key Symbols in the Holy Royal Arch Degree

GRAND CHAPTER ORGANIZATION

The Grand Chapter is the sovereign governing body of the four Capitular Degrees in each State. The General Grand Chapter, as we have seen above, is an advisory body to which most Chapters in the United States belong (some have never joined, due to a sense of individuality; while other have occasionally joined, left and joined again, depending upon the temperament of their ruling Officers). It also serves a function similar to the Council of Grand Masters, since every three years a Triennial is held at which the senior Officers of the States and Countries who are members of General Grand Chapter may come together to discuss ideas, resolve issues and generally fraternize.

The Grand Chapter is composed of Officers similar to those in a regular Chapter. Like Lodges, Chapters are grouped into Districts, each under a District Deputy Grand High Priest, who is the Grand High Priest's representative in that District, who makes annual visits to each Chapter to inspect its books and records, to deliver the Grand High Priest's message, and make a report on his District to Grand Chapter. Once a year Grand Chapter holds an Annual Communication. Traditionally this has been held in Albany, both because this is considered relatively central to the State, and also because it honors the tradition established in 1789 by Thomas Smith Webb, DeWitt Clinton, Ezra Ames and other early notable Companions who held their meetings there.

The Grand Chapter maintains a website at ny-royal-arch.org, at which useful announcements, as well as calendars of activities, forms and educational materials may be found.

At the Annual Communication business is discussed, reports of the Committees received, the Grand Treasurer and Grand Secretaries Reports approved, the Grand High Priest's decisions reviewed, and the Grand High Priest's annual address delivered. Proposed changes to the Constitution require two readings at two successive Annual Communications before being approved. Elections for the following year's Grand Line Officers are also held, and those elected are installed. Those entitled to vote include the Grand Line Officers, Past Elected Grand Line Officers, and the current High Priest, King and Scribe of each Chapter, so long as that Chapter is in good standing. For each Chapter the High Priest, King and Scribe should make every effort to attend the Annual Communication, or send a proxy (indeed every High Priest who has not been anointed is required to attend in order to participate in the Anointed High Priest Ceremony, without which he cannot serve as High Priest of a Chapter). Each Chapter is entitled to 3 votes plus 1 extra vote for every 50 members above the first 50. One very useful product of the Annual Communication is a Directory, which lists the Grand Line, Committee Members, District Officers and all the Chapters.

Each District has a District Deputy Grand High Priest, as previously mentioned; together with an Assistant Grand Lecturer, who is responsible for assisting the Chapter with their ritual learning, and organizing training in the District; and a Charity Chairman, who is responsible for organizing charity events in the District and monitoring the contributions from the Chapters.

In addition, as with Grand Lodge, a number of Grand Representatives are appointed at the Grand High Priest's pleasure, to serve as liaison with other jurisdictions and to represent their interests at our Grand Chapter.

The Grand Line comprises elected and appointed Officers. The elected Officers are:

- Grand High Priest
- Grand King
- Grand Scribe
- Grand Treasurer
- Grand Secretary

In addition there are a five elected Trustees.

The Appointed Officers are:

- Grand Captain of the Host
- Grand Principal Sojourner
- Grand Royal Arch Captain
- Grand Master of the Third Veil
- Grand Master of the Second Veil
- Grand Master of the First Veil
- Grand Sentinel

In addition there are other Appointed Officers, including the Judge Advocate, Grand Lecturer, Grand Chaplains, Grand Musicians, Grand Historian, and such other positions as the Grand High Priest may judge appropriate.

In addition there is a body called the Permanent Members Committee. This is composed of Past Grand High Priests and the Grand Council (sitting Grand High Priest, Grand King and Grand Scribe). This body meets at least twice a year and gives advice to the Grand Council, putting forward ideas, discussing experiences, and giving their approval to the line of Officers and the plans of the incoming Grand High Priest.

While most of these Officers and functions parallel those of Grand Lodge, there is one aspect in which the Grand Chapter is very different. This is the concept of the 'Permanent Six', or P6. Some time ago it was decided, in line with the other York Rite bodies, that having a progressive line would be a sensible way to encourage a continued high level of commitment from its members, and also to allow long range planning in the knowledge that a particular strategy will be adhered to over a period of years, to allow it to succeed. At the present time, the positions of the three Grand Masters of the Veils and, more recently, the Grand Sentinel, are seen as a 'proving ground'. Once they have served their term, they will be considered for the position of Grand Royal Arch Captain in the future if their year in office has proved exemplary. Once a Companion is believed by the existing Grand Line and the Permanent Committee to be a suitable Candidate for eventual Grand High Priesthood, that person is appointed by the incoming Grand High Priest to be Grand Captain of the Host. This person will normally continue automatically up through the next five offices to Grand High Priest.

A member of the Royal Arch is called a Companion, as was explained in the Ritual. A High Priest of a Chapter is given the title 'Excellent' or E∴. An Assistant Grand Lecturer is titled Very Excellent or V∴E∴. A District Deputy High Priest or any Grand Line Officer is a Right Excellent, or R∴E∴. Finally, a serving or former Grand High Priest is called Most Excellent, or M∴E∴.

Although it is not a hard and fast rule, most try to avoid the term ' *Past* High Priest' or *'Past* Grand High Priest'. The reason for this stems from the New Testament line "Thou art a priest forever, after the Order of Melchizedek" (Hebrews 7:17). Since the Anointed High Priest ceremony draws much of its symbolism from the story of Abram and Melchizedek in Genesis Chapter 14, the phrase 'Past' seems inappropriate. Normally, 'High Priest' or 'Grand High Priest' continue to be used even when that person is out of office.

BLUE AND RED MASONRY

While the preceding degrees are not completely monochromatic, it must have caught the attention of someone passing through those Degrees that color is not one of the major features of the Degrees. Light Blue is just about the only color seen before the Royal Arch (not counting the purple and gold Grand Lodge aprons in our jurisdiction). Indeed, in some traditions the aprons were black and white, so the experience of the early degrees was truly an experience without colors. Of course, early aprons including George Washington's show that this wasn't always the case. Still, the colors are certainly muted until this Degree, when the Chapter starts to field colorful banners in addition to the predominant color red, and of course the multicolored breastplate of the High Priest.

Quite often the banners are presented in what are known as 'complementary' or 'flashing' colors. These are colors which, when mixed, produce black or white. When put next to one another, they strongly reinforce each other, even appearing to flash. If one color is used as a background and the other as an image or word on it, the image or word appears to pop out of the flat background into three dimensions. The most often used colors are red and green, yellow and violet, and blue and orange. In Chapter, for example, the Blue banner will often have the name of the tribe in orange, and so forth.

Red, we are told, is the color of zeal. The first time the Candidate sees this color is when the blindfold is lifted for a moment and he sees the burning bush. From this first instant the Candidate is taught to associate zeal with God. Now if red is a 'hot' and 'zealous' color, blue is a 'cool' color, and readily identifies with the injunction to 'subdue my passions' in the first three Degrees. We must first learn self-control, so that our zeal comes from a calm center and is not merely hot-headedness.

In the past the first three Degrees were sometimes referred to as the Blue Degrees, and by inference took place in a Blue Lodge. The Royal Arch Degrees, which took the analogy into the more spiritual world were referred to as the Red Degrees, which took place in a Red Lodge. The four banners are Blue, Purple, Red and White. These are referred to the four principal tribes of Israel. They also express four levels of consciousness. On a more basic level they also indicate the four bodies of the York Rite itself. The color purple features strongly in the Cryptic Degrees, and white (as well as black) is the signal color associated with Chivalric Orders, in this case the Order of the Temple.

In modern Masonry the color purple is normally closely tied to blue, since it is an indication of rulership in the Craft.

Many Masonic Regimes make much of the colors Blue or Black, Red and White. For example, the Scottish Rectified Rite has three Blue Degrees, then one Red Degree, and finally two White Chivalric Degrees. In New York this pattern is also followed as the Cryptic Degrees are optional, and not a prerequisite to the Order of the Temple. One may therefore pass from Blue Lodge, through Red Chapter into White Chivalry.

On a symbolic level the progression from black through red to white indicates increasing zeal and also purification, since it follows the colors are a dark substance or metal is heated. Firstly it glows with a dull red, becoming brighter and brighter as the applied heat is intensified. Finally it glows white hot.

We find this closely reflects alchemical teaching, whose teachings attempted to raise a base substance to a higher level - traditionally base metal into gold. This was also an analogy of raising base and ignorant man to a higher level of purity and worthiness to unite with God. In this the teachings of spiritual alchemy and Freemasonry are not so dissimilar.

So the progress through the Veils during the ritual represents, on one level, a progressive raising from a lower level of existence to a higher plane or rarified level. Think about the meaning behind passing through four veils in order to be received into the presence of three superior beings, each reflecting an aspect of the divine (Omnipotence, Omniscience, Omnipresence). And this is but a different way of representing that spiritual journey we all undertook in the Blue Degree, when our progress was successively barred by the Junior and Senior Wardens. The first time we encountered them we had a guide, the Senior Deacon, a psychopomp who answered for us: but the next time we answered for ourselves.

CONTEXT OF THE HOLY ROYAL ARCH DEGREE

To most Brothers who experience the Holy Royal Arch Degree for the first time, it is a blur of colors, movement, stories, allegories, costumes, weird grips and positions, and little is remembered.

However, two hundred years ago, well-versed in the stories of the Bible as our members were, the stories being enacted would spark an immediate reaction in the Candidates. From their first steps into the Chapter they would already be thinking: "I know these stories so well. Now what messages are the Freemasons going to draw from them?"

So in a way we have a lot more catching up to do than our predecessors.

Another thing to remember is, in the earliest days of recorded Freemasonry, long before the many Orders and Degrees which tempt us now, there were the Blue degrees, the Mark Degree and the Royal Arch. This last Degree was considered the *ne plus ultra* of those early days, and so precious that no Mason who had not been installed as Master of his Lodge could even grasp its precepts. This Degree was seen either as the highest and most important Degree in Freemasonry; or a critical pivot Degree allowing a well-educated Mason to be prepared to enter the Chivalric Orders.

And what of those? The earliest forms of chivalry were a decidedly local honor, where the Lord of the Manor or Laird of the Castle would dub dedicated members of his staff with the title 'knight', who was then expected to defend the Castle and people who lived there. The troubadours raised this concept of honor and the love of an unattainable lady to the highest form of art and desirability, and over time the ability to create knights was arrogated to monarchs and popes. Orders such as the Poor Fellow-Soldiers of Christ and of the Temple of Solomon, better known to us as the Knights Templar, sprang up. Endorsed by the Papacy, it was still nevertheless the local Commanders and Preceptors who knighted the men under their charge. This concept of local knighting linked to a sense of apostolic or initiatory succession gives the Masonic Order of Knights Templar a real sense of being a 'true' knight.

From this one should realize that being Exalted to the Holy Royal Arch Degree is one of the most important events which will happen to you in Masonry, outside of receiving the Master Mason Degree. In one Degree you have *completed* the Master Mason Degree, learned the True Word, experienced that high honor which early Masons sought, and been given those tools and symbols which would bring you to a state worthy of being considered for knighthood!

Since knights were expected to be pure of mind and body, working on perfecting themselves to a high level of skill and physical fitness in the art of war, so we can see the analogy with the Blue Degrees. Similarly, as the knight was expected to be pure in thoughts and deeds, to hold all women and children sacred and under his protection, and to make vigil in the service of Christ, so the spiritual side of Masonry exemplified in the Red Degrees is seen.

And here we see an unavoidable historical fact: Europe was Christian, and the Orders of Chivalry were Christian. This story was considered so important, just about every Masonic system contains a Degree which focuses in some manner on the rebuilding of the destroyed Temple upon the foundation which survived. We see it in the Ancient Accepted Scottish Rite, the Irish Order of Knight Masons, the French Rectified Rite, and of course the Royal Arch Degree, to name just a few. In most it serves as a pivot Degree, which means it closes one cycle of Degrees, normally Old Testament, and opens a new cycle, normally based upon the New Testament.

However, whether the Degree focuses upon an avatar - Jesus of Nazareth - or the Candidate as a subject of spiritual alchemical transmutation, the message is the same: we all contain a spark of the divine, and by descending into ourselves, finding it and bringing it into consciousness, we can vivify the physical temple of our body on which we worked in the Blue Degrees, and bring it to spiritual life, becoming true knights among men, with a renewed sense of purpose towards our fellow man, understanding the symbolic injunctions of the knights of old, and bringing that sense of respect and service back into our lives.

Your first meeting following the Degree should hopefully be the Walkabout, which reviews the Officers and equipment of a Chapter, and this is a first step to begin to unravel the deep meaning behind this immense Degree.

KEY SYMBOLS IN THE HOLY ROYAL ARCH DEGREE

In the Bible God did not speak directly to mankind very often. If He wished to communicate He normally did this through prophets, and occasionally through angels. If we review the Pentateuch, or first five Books of the Bible, also known as the Books of Moses since tradition has it that Moses authored them, or at least passed the knowledge on to his successors, God first spoke to Adam and Eve. Outside of Eden, after man's fall, we see He also communicated directly with Cain, and with Noah when he wished to save him. The next time God spoke directly to man it was to Moses from the burning bush. This is also the first time He gave his Name, rather than asking Cain after Abel, or instructing Noah how to save himself and his family. This is significant, since in Genesis God told Adam to name the animals which, as we have seen, in esoteric language implies he is master over them. By telling Moses His name, God gave Moses an important gift: the power to summon Him. In Moses' several encounters with God on the Mount and during his travels in the wilderness, the conversations show that God and Moses had what amounted to two-way conversations.

The first thing the Candidate sees in the Chapter Room, when his blindfold is removed, is the burning bush, and he is told that God gave his true Name to Moses. At the very start of the Ritual he is presented with the fact that the True Masons Word involves God, thought at this point he does not comprehend it. This is rather like that moment in the Entered Apprentice's Lodge when upon his first entrance into the Lodge the Candidate stands, blindfolded, between the two pillars yet because of the blindfolded, cannot see this. Standing there he is the Middle Pillar standing between the Pillars of Severity and Mercy and balancing them. And he will spend his entire Masonic career trying to reach this point of perfect equilibrium once more, but this time in full possession of his faculties, without a blindfold. Similarly in the Royal Arch, symbolically he will become the Keystone he encountered in the Mark Master Degree, uniting the two pillars and binding those two opposites together, uniting them once more.

In the Most Excellent Master Degree six circuits, or circumambulations are performed by the Candidate, accompanied by readings from the Old Testament. This time there are seven circumambulations. This time, however, each circuit is linked to an actual historical event involving physical relocation. While the first circuit is predominantly a tradition challenge: "Who comes here?" issued this time by the Captain of the Host, the six subsequent circumambulations reflect successive events in history where the Israelites or their leaders were forced to travel.

2nd Circuit - Moses goes to Mount Horeb and sees the burning bush
3rd Circuit - Moses goes back to Egypt to preach to the Israelites
4th Circuit - The Israelites leave Egypt and wander in the desert for forty years
5th Circuit - The Israelites cross over the Jorden and enter the Promised Land
6th Circuit - The Israelites are subdued and taken into captivity East to Babylon
7th Circuit - Following Cyrus' proclamation the Israelites travel West back to the Promised Land

We see this time the circuits are not used to represent the days of creation, but periods of unrest and movement.

The Most Excellent Master Degree ended with stability, for we were taught in the Blue Degree that the two conjoined Pillars stood for Stability, "for the Lord said: 'In strength will I establish this mine house to stand firm forever.'" (at least this is what the Ritual says, but there is no record of this in the Scriptures). The seven circuits therefore represents periods of unrest and instability. Finally, the Royal Arch Degree gives us our second period of extended stability, with the erection of the Second Temple upon the ruins of the First.

The weary Sojourners arrive at the entrance to the Tabernacle, or the temporary housing which was used by Moses in the wilderness. Again we see the transition from impermanence or instability to permanence or stability. The Tabernacle represented the temporal residence of the Divine, until a permanent place could be built in Jerusalem. Now that was destroyed, He again dwells in an impermanent home until the enduring Temple can be built once more.

As a final point for contemplation, it is interesting to note the great importance not only associated with the number '3', as we have seen throughout Masonry, but specifically with the idea that three are required to be present and agree to do something, in order for that action to be efficacious. Matthew 18:20 quotes Jesus as saying: "For where two or three are gathered together in my name, there am I in the midst of them." We hear this phrase in a number of our prayers, for example in Opening a Lodge. The meaning is clear: if two - but especially three - gather together, what they are doing will meet with success.

As we pass through the Veils we learn of several groups of three men who accomplished great tasks. Shem, Ham and Japheth were the sons of Noah (Genesis 6:10), who assisted him in building the Ark which saved the remnants of humanity from the flood. This Ark was a great vessel which contained men, women and animals. Incidentally, Moses was left in a tiny ark among the bulrushes where he was discovered by the Egyptian princess (Exodus 2:3). The inclusion of Noah's sons in this Ritual is probably partly because they built the first ark or container; but also because the story of Noah's Ark featured strongly in early Masonic ritual (called the "Royal Ark Mariner Degree"), and may be one of the sources which ended up being incorporated into part of the Royal Arch Degree.

Another clue can be found in the first few Chapters of I Chronicles. In one of those 'A begat B' lists we often find in the earlier books of the Bible, the line of succession is carefully traced from Adam to Noah and his three sons. It is then made clear that the progeny of Seth led to Abraham, and then to David and Solomon. It goes further to race the line down through to Zerubbabel. So the passage through the Veils, in addition to many other meanings, also refers to the passage of Jewish history, from the antediluvian period up to the time of the rebuilding of the Temple, and identifies four great trios of builders: the sons who built the Ark (Ham, Shem and Japheth); those who formed the First or Holy Lodge, and were responsible for creating the Tabernacle and its furniture, including the Ark of the Covenant - Moses, Aholiab and Bezaleel; then Solomon, Hiram King of Tyre and Hiram Abif who formed the Sacred Lodge, and oversaw the erection of the Temple; and finally Zerubbabel, Jeshua and Haggai, who formed the Royal Lodge, and superintended the reconstruction of the Temple.

Of course the most important point of three coming together is learned at the end of the Degree, and perhaps surprisingly for the Candidate it is a physical as well as verbal act, which was hinted at with the giving of the Substitute Word between only two people in the Master Mason Degree. At last, we learn why only two gave that Word, and why it could not be given after Hiram's death until the rediscovery of the True Word, and why this word can now be given in such a powerful manner.

The Royal Arch Degree is arguably the most powerful, most complete, most spiritual and most educational of all the Degrees. Certainly, Laurence Dermott, Grand Secretary of the Antients thought so when he called it the 'root, heart and marrow of Freemasonry.'

We sincerely hope that, as you study the Degree, and those which precede it, you will be led to the same conclusion.

Session 5
(This should be at the first meeting following the conferral of the Holy Royal Arch Degree)

INTRODUCTION

Now the Candidate has completed the Royal Arch Cycle of Degrees, and the new Companion is entitled to sit in a Chapter, some information about the Chapter is given, including the Officers and key furnishings, so that he does not feel uncomfortable in his new surroundings.

Other opportunities for the Candidate to increase his Masonic knowledge in Royal Arch Masonry are reviewed. This includes both courses offered by Grand Chapter and other options, including the excellent reading courses offered by the Chancellor Robert R. Livingston Library.

The Chapter Walkabout is the culmination of the new Companion's training. In it both the key symbols in the Chapter and the roles of the Officers are explained. Perhaps more importantly, he will be taken round the Chapter to meet its most active members. These are people who will answer questions and mentor the new Companion in the future.

Finally, the avenues available to the new Companion are identified. Being a Master Mason is the most important title anyone has in Freemasonry; but being a Royal Arch Mason opens a bewildering number of new Orders a Mason may join. Most are invitational, but the rest of the York Rite is open to anyone who is a Companion and expresses a desire to join.

FIFTH SESSION SUBJECTS

1. Chapter Organization
2. Further Education Opportunities
3. The Chapter Walkabout
4. Whither now?

CHAPTER ORGANIZATION

The Chapter is organized around nine key Officers. Perhaps the most unusual difference in the Chapter to a Lodge is the fact that it is ruled by three people in the East, the High Priest, King and Scribe. You have seen in the Royal Arch Degree that the functions of the King and Scribe are minimal, and one may have expected them to fulfil the roles of Senior and Junior Wardens. However, you have seen that the function of Senior Warden is in fact filled by the Captain of the Host; while the Royal Arch Captain fills the seat of the Junior Deacon who answers the knocks made by the Sentinel. Also, the Principal Sojourner is responsible for attending at the Altar. These, along with the three Masters of the Veils, compose the nine Officers. The other three position are the Treasurer, Secretary and the Sentinel, who stands guard outside the outer door.

These Officers are arranged in three groups of three, just as they are when they form the Royal Arch, the Three Principal Officers in the extreme East, followed by the three secondary Officers; and the three Masters of the Veils in the far West (always with the most Senior Officer in the East):

1. High Priest
2. King
3. Scribe

4. Captain of the Host
5. Principal Sojourner
6. Royal Arch Captain

7. Master of the Third Veil
8. Master of the Second Veil
9. Master of the First Veil

Why are there three Officers in the East? In the Ritual they represent the three leaders of the Israelites: the High Priest, the King and the Scribe or Prophet. In other jurisdictions the King is the senior Officer, but in most of the United States it is the High Priest. As we heard in the opening they represent Jeshua, the High Priest, Zerubbabel, the King, and Haggai, the Scribe or Prophet.

We know that these three roles were critical in the organizational structure of Ancient Egypt. The King was both ruler and god; the Priests held power and tended to the spiritual needs of the people, while the scribes represented the legal side of daily life, both recording events and issuing regulations. However, by the time this model had been taken to the Promised Land, into exile and back to Israel once more, the role of King was to some extent diminished, and we might see the role more as figurehead, a rallying point. This is expressly made clear in the biblical stories around the exile in Babylon. It is not the king who leads the people, since King Jehoiakin had been discredited and his sons killed before his eyes at the destruction of Jerusalem by Nebuzaradan, and it is hard to rule when you have no kingdom. So Zerubbabel could only claim an indirect line to the throne. On the other hand it was the prophets and priests who had to keep up the flagging spirits of the exiled Israelites, and exhort them to maintain their faith and offer prophecies of better times, when God would forgive them and allow them to return to their homeland. Remember, too, that as well as the prevarication of Kings, it was through turning away from the Priests and Prophets that the Israelites believed they had lost their Promised Land.

On a more spiritual level the three rulers or High Council are emblems of three key aspects of our own makeup: body, soul and spirit. The King wields temporal power, and therefore represents all that is earthly and holds on to life. The Prophet is the link with the higher realm, and represents that inner yearning to reunite with God. The Priest represents that sacred side of us which leads us through inner contemplation and prayer to be one with God. It is interesting that these three aspects are separated out into three distinct personalities. However, we should also note that they only become fully effective when reunited, when they form the Royal Arch in order to confer the Degree or utter the True and Sacred Name of God. In the English (or Domatic) Ritual, the three Principals come together to form the Arch. Each one individually says an attribute of God: 'Omnipotent',

'Omniscient', 'Omnipresent', before uttering together 'God'. It is the moment when the three fuse into one, representing man's ability to utter the Name – and therefore summon – God.

These form the first triumvirate of Officers.

The second trio are the Captain of the Host, the Principal Sojourner, and the Royal Arch Captain. They sit in front of the Principal Officers, with the Royal Arch Captain to the side. In a way their offices reflect those of the principal Officers, but while the High Priest, King and Scribe almost never move from their positions, only coming down to the floor to inspect the Ark and confer the Word; and the three Masters of the Veil remains at their posts, these three Officers move freely about the Chapter. As we saw earlier the Captain of the Host and Royal Arch Captain fulfill functions of Senior Warden and Junior Deacon, while the Principal Sojourner moves freely around the Chapter leading the Candidates, not unlike a Senior Deacon or Marshall.

The third trio are the Masters of the Veils, who also represent the three Sojourners who returned from Babylon and proved their worth through an act of humility. Despite being worthy of coming before the presence of the High Council and bearing the personal ring of Zerubbabel, which would indicate they were high born, they do not reject the most menial tasks, working among the rubbish of the fallen Temple. There they make those important discoveries, and both for their work and their humility they are 'exalted' to become the Masters of the Veils. And the ceremony of becoming a Companion is also called 'Exaltation' for that very reason. Remember the first words uttered when you entered the room: "He that humblest himself shall be exalted" (Matthew 23:12 and Luke 14:11).

The three principal Officers sit in the East, the three Masters of the Veils along the South, and the other three in a triangle in the East.

FURTHER EDUCATION OPPORTUNITIES

Now you have completed the cycle of Capitular Degrees, the same injunction may be given that you received at the end of the Master Mason Degree. These Degrees are not intended to be experienced once. They are to be watched, examined, and contemplated often. The more you study them the more that effort will be repaid in insights and life lessons.

The first way, therefore to further educate yourself is to attend your Chapter regularly, where, if you are lucky, you will have the opportunity to see the Degrees put on at least once a year. If not, what are you doing to ensure that happens? Join the line, participate, and offer to do the Lectures, the Working Tools, be an Overseer. The best way to understand a Ritual is by participating in it. If your Chapter makes a point of having lectures during the year, consider yourself fortunate indeed. If not, why not invite Companions you know who are educated in the Degrees to come and speak? There is even a series of Chapter Talking Points in the Education Session to get the Companions thinking – and talking. Attend the Grand Lecturer's Convention, and if the Grand Line are holding an event, Seminar or Symposium in your area make every attempt to attend.

Further, join Thomas Smith Webb Chapter of Research No. 1798. It is considered to be one of the foremost Research Chapters, and they meet across the State several times a year. If you are near another State visit a Chapter there: your extra effort will be more than repaid in terms of enjoying the slight variations in the local ritual landmarks, and the new friends you will make.

At the first meeting following your Exaltation you should experience the Chapter Walkabout, in which you are taken about the Chapter to meet the various Officers, who will explain their function, and also shown the Chapter furniture. If they cannot do this, speak to your District AGL to find another Chapter which is doing it soon.

Once you feel comfortable with the Chapter and its Rituals, consider going on to take the Capitular Development Course. This builds upon what you have learned, and takes the symbolism to a far greater depth. You will study the Ritual and also review the stories from which they are taken in your copy of the Volume of the Sacred Law.

Another great source of learning is the Chancellor Robert R. Livingston Library courses. There is a course specifically on the Royal Arch Degrees. Go to www.nymasoniclibrary.org/the-library and click on Reading Courses on the left side menu. Also, General Grand Chapter (www.ramint.org) has an excellent Four Volume series entitled History of Royal Arch Masonry which are very comprehensive and cover origins of the Degrees, as well as the Development of Royal Arch in the United States and elsewhere.

Further education may be found on the Internet. For example, the Sovereign York Rite College offer an interesting course. Their *Companion Adept of the Temple* course can be found on the Forms page of their website (www.yrscna.org). However, this course covers all the York Rite Bodies, and would only be useful to those who possess the Cryptic Degrees and Templar Orders too. Beyond this, there are many books and monitors available which will further open up the mysteries of these Degrees to those who seek.

The text of the Chapter Walkabout, which your Chapter should endeavor to offer once you have become a Royal Arch Mason, is reproduced below for your reference.

THE CHAPTER WALKABOUT

The Chapter is set up as for the Opening Ceremony. In particular, as well as the usual Stations, the Banners (including the Royal Arch Banner), the Altar and Great Lights, care should be taken to ensure the Royal Arch Captain is in possession of a Signet Ring preferably bearing the traditional 'Yod', that the Charter is prominently displayed, and that a copy of the Constitutions and Bylaws are close at hand. Finally, on the Trestleboard table there should be a candlestick bearing a white candle, and a red taper on the Secretary's desk.

The newly exalted Companions should be seated in the North East. Once the Chapter has been Opened, any business should be undertaken so that the Chapter Walkabout Ceremony is the last item on the Agenda before the Closing. It is important that the explanations to the newly exalted Companions should not be obscured by business.

It is suggested that the King runs the evening, but if the Chapter so wishes the High Priest – or the Scribe – can take the King's part instead. The reason for this is to allow the King to have an active role in the year before he is High Priest; he should have the time to organize and rehearse the Walkabout Ceremony, leaving the High Priest to focus on running the Chapter and conferring the Degrees. The King (High Priest or Scribe) may stand at a pedestal on the dais in the East and read his part: it is highly recommended that all the other parts are done from memory.

King Companion Principal Sojourner (*PS rises and salutes*), cause the newly exalted Companions to stand before me.

PS goes to the North East (with stick) and asks the newly exalted Companions to rise and follow him. He leads them before the King, facing East in a line, and remains standing at the right end of the line.

PS Companion King, the newly exalted Companions are assembled before you.

King My Companions, I welcome you into this Chapter of Royal Arch Masons. The purpose of this evening is to provide an explanation of key points of our ceremonies, the roles of the Officers and the furniture in our Chapter. You have progressed through the four degrees under the purview of the Grand Chapter of the State of New York, which culminated in your being exalted to the rank of Companion of the Holy Royal Arch; and this evening you have (for the first time) witnessed the Opening of the Chapter. I am sure that both the ceremony of your exaltation and the peculiarity of this evening's Opening have raised questions in your minds. It is our intention to answer some of those questions this evening.

The York Rite of Masonry is a progressive system of degrees in which the candidate for its mysteries has more and more light revealed with each successive grade. While the first three degrees, called Blue Lodge Masonry, bind us in a universal bond with our Brethren across the globe, we are privileged to be a part of an ancient English system which comprised a series of degrees, of which the first three form only part. Indeed, the purpose of these further grades, as you now know, were to complete the story begun in the first three degrees, and discover and bring to light the true word which was lost in the third degree. This journey took you through the discovery of the Keystone, and the ceremonies to mark the completion of King Solomon's Temple. You also underwent the ceremony of Passing the Chair in the Virtual Past Master's degree, to remind you that during its early history the privilege of receiving the degree of the Holy Royal Arch was only open to those who had been Masters of a Blue Lodge. Finally, you found yourself moving forward in history, past the golden years of Jerusalem and the Temple, when the Israelites obeyed God's just laws, past their prevarication and the awful punishment of seeing their Holy City reduced to rubble and being scattered abroad or led into captivity in Babylon, to that time when, under a more benign ruler, the Israelites were permitted to return to their homeland to rebuild their city and temple.

Symbolically, too, you moved from a Lodge where you were taught the importance of the horizontal, the perpendicular and the square, to a Chapter where the triangle and the arc are introduced. These are symbolized both by the Ark of the Covenant and the arc of the circle which forms the keystone. God's presence at our ceremonies is now represented by the Shekinah which replaces the letter 'G'. That which was implicit in the Blue Masonry are now made explicit in Red Masonry, and that which was veiled, represented by the Lost Work, is unveiled and restored to us.

The Ark and the Arch share a common linguistic root, and both remind us of Noah's ship upon the waters and the Ark of the Covenant borne across the expanse of the Sinai desert. The arch also reminds us of God's promise after the flood, and in many traditions the rainbow and ark, and the arch of Enoch are some of the earliest themes in Masonry. The Veils we see in the Chapter also reflect one of the earliest themes in what is called Capitular Masonry which simply means Masonry in a Chapter. They remind us that long before the Temple was built, a series of colored veils intervened between the people and the Ark within the confines of the tabernacle, which was used to house the Ark of the Covenant during its journey across the desert.

We will now proceed to review those symbols, and the duties which comprise our unique heritage.

As is customary, Companions, before entering upon this, or any other important undertaking, we will invoke the aid of Deity. (*Gavels three times ***). Give your attention to the Chaplain.

Chap   (*OPENING PRAYER*) Almighty God, unto whom all hearts are open, all desires, known, and from whom no secrets are hid, cleanse the thoughts of our hearts by the inspiration of Thy Holy Spirit, that we may truly love Thee and worthily magnify Thy Great and Sacred Name. Amen.

All   So Mote It Be.

King   * (*Companions, except the newly exalted Companions and the Principal Sojourner, are seated*). Companion Captain of the Host.

CH   Companion King.

King   Light the Shekinah.

CH   Companion Principal Sojourner.

PS   Companion Captain of the Host.

CH   Light the Shekinah.

PS goes to Secretary's Desk, finds and lights red taper there. Proceeds south, around the Altar, to the East where he lights the white taper. He puts out the red taper and places it beside the white taper. He then returns to his seat, passing West of the Altar. He should walk slowly and make right angles whenever changing direction. He returns to his position to the right of the newly-exalted Companions.

PS   Companion Captain of the Host.

CH   Companion Principal Sojourner.

PS   The Shekinah is present.

CH   Companion King.

King   Companion Captain of the Host.

CH   The flame, representing the presence of the Living God, is lit.

King   Companion Principal Sojourner.

PS   Companion King.

King   Conduct our new companions to the outer part of the Tabernacle, that they my pass by the Veils to receive instruction.

The PS tells the new Companions to right face, and follow him as he conducts them, with his stick, down the North side of the room behind the Veils. When he reaches the West he leads them to the center of the Western end of the room, then proceed up the center towards the First Veil. He halts before the First Veil, then turns to the new Companions and says:

PS   While the workmen who had returned from captivity in Babylon under the suffrage of King Cyrus rebuilt the ruined Temple, they held a trowel in one hand and a sword in the other, to partake in the work of rebuilding the walls but also being every ready to defend themselves against marauders and those who did not wish to see the Holy City and Temple rebuilt. Jeshua, Zerubbabel and Haggai, the members of the Grand Masonic Council, caused a tabernacle to be erected next to the building site, and held their meetings there. To safeguard themselves from being taken unawares by attacks or by eavesdroppers they posted guards at each of the four Veils which successively gave entrance to each court. The Veils were colored Blue, Purple, Red and White respectively, and as you will recall at your exaltation, in order to pass each one you were required to give a password, and in most cases a sign which accompanied it, in order to gain admission to the next Veil. Let us now approach the Master of the First Veil for instruction.

The PS now leads the new Companions to the M1V who rises, takes his banner in his right hand, and says:

M1V　　The distinctive color of Blue is an emblem of universal friendship and benevolence and instructs us that, in the mind of a Mason, those virtues should be as expansive as the blue arch of heaven itself. My pass is I Am That I Am, and refers to the name given by the Almighty to Moses when He spoke to him from within the burning bush.

The M1V returns his banner, while the PS leads the new Companions to the 2V who rises, takes his banner in hand, and says:

M2V　　The color Purple admonishes us to cultivate and improve that spirit of union and harmony between the brethren of the symbolic degrees and the Companions of the sublime degree which should ever distinguish the members of a society founded upon the principles of everlasting truth and universal philanthropy. My words are Shem, Ham and Japheth, the sons of Noah, and my sign is an imitation of that given by the Lord unto Moses when He commanded him to cast his rod upon the ground, whereupon it became a serpent, and devoured the rods of the Pharoah's magi.

The M2V returns his banner, while the PS leads the new Companions to the M3V who rises, takes his banner in hand, and says:

M3V　　The color Scarlet admonishes us to be fervent in the exercise of our devotion to God and zealous in our endeavors to promote the happiness of man. My words are Moses, Aholiab and Bezaleel, the three who were, respectively, responsible for governing the Israelites during their wanderings in the desert, the construction of the Ark of the Covenant, and of the Tabernacle in which it resided. My sign is an imitation of that given by the Lord unto Moses when he commanded him to place his hand in his bosom, and drew it out leprous. He then placed his hand once more into his bosom and when he withdrew it had turned again as his other flesh. I also give you this ring or signet, with which you will be able to gain admission to the Grand Council.

The M3V returns his banner, while the PS leads the new Companions to the RAC who rises, takes his banner in hand, and says:

RAC　　The color White signifies that purity of heart and rectitude of conduct which are so essential to live a good and true life. Present me the ring (*Done*). This eternal circle of gold is that of Zerubbabel, and represents Truth. My words are Jeshua, Zerubbabel, and Haggai, and are the names of the Grand Council, being the High Priest, King and Scribe. My sign is an imitation of that given by the Lord unto Moses when he commanded him to pour water on dry land, which appeared to turn to blood when Moses did as the Lord had commanded before Pharaoh. You now pass on into the Sanctuary, where in the ceremony of exaltation were to be found the triangular altar, together with the seven-branched candlestick and the altar of incense furnished by King Cyrus. However, in a regular meeting the candlestick, altar of incense and Ark of the Covenant are not present (*the RAC returns his banner*).

King The Principal Sojourner performs a dual role within the Chapter. Similar to the Senior Deacon in Blue Lodge, as representative of the High Priest he performs the duties at the Altar, leads devotions, and also conducts the Candidates along the path to enlightenment.

The Captain of the Host fulfills a function similar to that of the Senior Warden in Blue Lodge. When the Chapter is in session he sits in the throne at the West, and communicates the commands of the High Priest to the Companions, ensures those seeking to enter the Sanctuary have been duly processed and obligated, and is responsible for the security of the Chapter.

The Scribe represents Haggai and I, as King, represent Zerubbabel. The High Priest represents Jeshua, and it is the duty of the Scribe and King to assist the High Priest in his duties and to preside in his absence.

(*Indicates the Altar*) The equilateral or perfect triangle was adopted by the ancients as a symbol of the Deity – as embracing in Himself the three stages of time – the Past, the Present and the Future.

The number three has always been held in high esteem by the Fraternity. Indeed, at our Opening and at our Closing, we perform that very ceremony which in the Third Degree King Solomon and Hiram King of Tyre were unable to complete because of the death of Hiram Abif. We join together in a living triangle by foot and hands, in order to utter the True Word of Master Mason. Now you understand why the number three has always been of such great importance to all Royal Arch Masons.

The Altar is used as a base on which is placed the Great Light in Masonry. Upon it rest the Great Lights in Masonry, as in the preceding Degrees.

(*Indicates the Warrant, which should be prominently displayed*) Your attention is also directed to the Warrant issued by the Grand Chapter of the State of New York, Royal Arch Masons, which gives us the authority to meet and to confer degrees.

The HP rises, and the K indicates the breastplate he wears.

King This Breastplate is an imitation of that worn by the High Priest of Israel. The twelve stones allude to the twelve tribes of Israel. It is to teach you that you are always to bear in mind your responsibility to the laws and ordinances of the Institution and that the honor and interests of your Chapter and its members should be always in your heart.

Behind the Grand Council hangs the Royal Arch Banner, which bears a great cross of green edged with gold, and within each quarter we see the standards of the four principal tribes of Israel: the lion of Judah, the man of Reuben, the ox of Ephraim and the eagle of Dan. These potent symbols contain many interpretations, which will become clearer to you are you progress in your studies. The shield is supported by two Cherubim, and we also read the motto 'Holiness to the Lord', which we read in Exodus were the words placed upon a plate of gold affixed to the miter of Aaron, the first High Priest of Israel.

(*Indicates the candle*) The Shekinah first appeared as Moses consecrated the Tabernacle in the Wilderness. The Shekinah, a visible cloud of light, hovering over the Mercy Seat, was ever present over the Ark as it was seated in the Temple of Solomon. With the destruction of that edifice, the Shekinah has not since appeared. The single light in the East, the White Candle, symbolizes the Divine Presence giving light and power to our Royal Craft and is essential to its existence. As the disappearance of the Shekinah Light from the Ark of the Covenant signified the withdrawal of the Divine Presence, so in like manner the disappearance of Divine Power from this or any other Chapter, would presage the same sad, disastrous ending. The Charge is Clear. It is for us to see that, like Israel, we do not become vain-glorious by reason of our material accomplishments and wander after false gods, losing the Great Light, the Lesser Lights and the Shekinah.

The Holy Royal Arch lifts the veil and brings each votary face to face with eternal Truth. The Great I AM. Everyone that enters the Sanctuary of the Tabernacle finds much beyond the limits of Craft Masonry without which their Masonic Life would be incomplete. May the Light of Almighty God shine forever upon us in the noble and glorious work in which we are engaged.

And now, my newly-exalted Companions, I hope that our explanations had helped you to understand the symbols and the roles within the Chapter, and that your future visits to our meetings will be full of teaching and enjoyment. I cannot stress strongly enough the importance to preserving this unique piece of Masonic ritual history, which has been described as the "heart, root, backbone and marrow of Freemasonry." Study its complex symbols, take part in its meetings, take office in the Chapter, and your endeavors will be rewarded beyond measure. And now my companions, give your attention to the Chaplain. *** (*All rise*).

Chap   Let us pray. Gracious God, we thank Thee for this education, and beseech Thee to guide and direct this Chapter and its members day by day so that they may be a faithful example of the meaning and significance of both faith and fraternity in the world. Amen.

All   So mote it be.

King   * Companion Principal Sojourner, escort our newly-exalted Companions to their seats (*done*).

WHITHER NOW?

You have now completed a Degree which, in conjunction with the Master Mason Degree, opens up many doors in Freemasonry to you, should you desire to continue your journey through the Orders. By taking the first steps into the wider family of Freemasonry you are becoming aware that there is much more to offer the curious mind 'beyond the Craft' as one book titles it. There are many organizations which may appeal to you whatever you seek.

Be aware that not all of those which follow will be available in your area or State. This list is not comprehensive, but there are enough Orders to get you started as you search the Internet or read books.

Within the York Rite the Cryptic Rite is available to all Companions, and the Order of the Temple to those who can commit to certain Christian vows.

There is an entire complimentary branch of Masonry called the Ancient Accepted Scottish Rite, which is composed of 33 Degrees. Both the Northern and Southern Masonic Jurisdictions' sites deserve a visit, and there are several courses to which you can subscribe.

For those who wish to serve more in charitable roles there is the Shrine, the Grotto, and the Tall Cedars of Lebanon.

Those attracted to Co-Masonry which is approved by Free & Accepted Masons may seek out the Order of the Eastern Star and the Order of the Amarinth. If already a Knight Templar, one's Lady may wish to enlist in the Order of the Beauceant. Sons may find a home in the Order of DeMolay, and daughters in the International Order of Rainbow Girls, the Order of Triangles or Job's Daughters International.

Education can continue in the many correspondence courses available, as well as excellent monthly magazines, such as *Living Stones*, which is one of the best (living-stones-magazine.myshopify.com). Other organization such as the Masonic Society provide valuable magazines (www.themasonicsociety.com). There are many Facebook, Google and other sites, but exercise the usual caution you would when visiting unstructured or unaudited sites: they can contain dangerous misinformation.

Beyond this there are many Invitational Orders, meaning simply that someone has to invite you to join. Some are research-oriented like the American Lodge of Research and the Allied Masonic Degrees. Others are spiritual in nature, including the SRICF (Societas Rosicruciana in Civitatibus Foederatis), the Order of Spiritual Knights, and so forth. Further chivalry continues in the Commemorative Order of St. Thomas of Acon. Then there are the Operatives, the Red Cross of Constantine, the York Rite College, Knight Templar Priests. The list is an endless as the time you have to spare!

But almost all of them begin with the step you have just taken.

www.ingramcontent.com/pod-product-compliance
Lightning Source LLC
Chambersburg PA
CBHW080940030426
42339CB00008B/470